D1379742

SERMON
OUTLINES
FROM
SERMON
MASTERS—

Old Testament

IAN MACPHERSON

SERMON OUTLINES FROM SERMON MASTERS—Old Testament

ABINGDON PRESS
NEW YORK
NASHVILLE

SERMON OUTLINES FROM SERMON MASTERS—

OLD TESTAMENT

Copyright © 1962 by Abingdon Press

Library of Congress Catalog Card Number: 60-5474

SET UP, PRINTED, AND BOUND BY THE
PARTHENON   PRESS,   AT   NASHVILLE,
TENNESSEE, UNITED STATES OF AMERICA

PREFACE

*P*REACHERS ARE PRONE TO two errors in preparing their sermons. One is to make too little of the plan, the other to make too much of it.

Some make too little of it. Trying to find the spine of their pulpit speech is like looking for the backbone of a fog. As one listens to their allocutions one is irresistibly reminded of the remark of Theseus in the play on the theatrical performance of Quince the carpenter: "This fellow doth not stand upon points."

Ours is an eminently practical age, an age in a hurry, an age tartly impatient of all vagueness, indeterminacy, circumlocution. "Boneless sermons stewed in cream"—to quote Professor Slosson's fulsome phrase—are completely out of fashion. People nowadays want to know at once what a preacher is driving at. Above all else, they want him to be clear; and they very properly feel that clarity begins at home, and that if a man's ideas are not plain to himself it is highly improbable that he will succeed in putting them over plainly to others.

But how are they to become plain to himself? That is the crucial question. One of the best ways of securing this is to start by drafting a plan; getting down, as it were, to the bare bones of things, and finally fitting the bones together with orthopedic care. Having such an outline luminously printed on his mind, the preacher is much less likely to grow mistily mysterious or to pour forth vaporings as invertebrate as a gas.

A cynical critic of the pulpit has said: "The traditional sermons used to possess three points, the more modern sermon only one point, and the ultra-modern no point at all!" Almost certainly, for speaker and hearers alike, a discourse without points will be a discourse without point. Some make too little of the plan.

Others, however, make too much of it. Their sermons are monstrosities, with divisions and subdivisions galore. At them Joseph Parker tilts delightfully in *Ad Clerum:*

> Some preachers are outline mad. They are nothing but outline. They plan beautifully, but build nothing. Give them the word "thinking" as a text, and they will see in it:
> 1) Man is a reduced physical state.
>   "Thin."
> 2) Man in a high social state.
>   "King."
> 3) Man in a truly intellectual state.
>   "Thinking."

To a pulpiteer of this type one is fain to say: "If thy heads offend thee, cut them off and cast them from thee."

Well, there is a happy medium between a ghost and a skeleton. And it is that—a living, breathing body —which the preacher should take as a model in the making of his sermons.

This further selection of *Sermon Outlines from Sermon Masters* owes its origin to the generous welcome accorded to the former; and in particular to the "enthusiastic interest" of a reader who kindly wrote to the publisher suggesting the issue of a companion volume of Old Testament plans. For this friendly encouragement one feels unspeakably grateful and trusts that the present collection will not disappoint the hopes of those thus indirectly responsible for its production.

How easy it would have been to have made the book many times its size! So inexhaustibly ample are the available materials that the temptation was strong to let the work grow to far greater proportions. The temptation was resisted for two reasons. One was the desire to keep this little volume uniform with the earlier book of New Testament outlines. The other was the realization that a slim book of this sort could be slipped comfortably into the pocket and so become a vade mecum in which the preacher might browse as he moved about in the course of his duties. Contemplating this collection of homiletic outlines, one's impulse is to echo the prophetic conjuration of Ezekiel: "Come from the four winds, O breath, and breathe upon these [bones], that they may live."

IAN MACPHERSON

CONTENTS

GENESIS

1. PEERING INTO THE PREHISTORIC PAST

"In the beginning God." GEN. 1:1

I once visited a great exhibition in which there was a planetarium. With a feeling of wonder mingled with awe, I stood on a railed platform, looking out, as it seemed, into infinity and watching fairly large models of the spheres—made and placed in the little firmament according to scale—whirling in their orbits.

That is the sort of sensation with which we read these words. "In the beginning God." No argument, simply a statement of fact. And as we peer into the prehistoric past, what do we see?

1. We see mystery penetrated by Mind.
2. We see form activated by force.
3. We see space interfused with Spirit.

2. TRACING THINGS TO THEIR SOURCE

"In the beginning God created the heaven and the earth." GEN. 1:1

This explanation of origins is:

1. Simple
2. Sublime
3. Sufficient

—Joseph Parker

3. THE HATCHING OF THE WORLDS

"The Spirit of God [brooded] upon the face of the waters." GEN. 1:2

What a magnificent picture of creation! The Spirit

11

of God, like a great bird, warming the worlds into existence.

1. Like a bird, the Spirit broods lovingly.
2. Like a bird, the Spirit broods vitalizingly.
3. Like a bird, the Spirit broods patiently.

4. THE GIST OF GENESIS

1. Generation
    "And God said, Let us make man in our image." Gen. 1:26
2. Degeneration
    "And God saw that the wickedness of man was great in the earth." Gen. 6:5
3. Regeneration
    "And God remembered Noah, and every living thing." Gen. 8:1

—George Campbell Morgan

5. THE GREAT CHARTER

And God said, Let us make man in our image, after our likeness: and let them have dominion."

Gen. 1:26

1. Man exercises his sovereignty in the world instinctively, that is, without conscious reflection.
2. Man also exercises his delegated sovereignty over all the earth through science.
3. Man exercises his sovereignty even more wonderfully in art.
4. Man exercises his sovereignty most effectively only through true religion, or the life in God.

—James Denney, The Way Everlasting

6. DOUBLES

"And God said, Let us make man in our image, after our likeness." Gen. 1:26
"And Adam . . . begat a son in his own likeness, after his image." Gen. 5:3
"[Christ] who is the image of the invisible God."

Col. 1:15

"God sending his own Son in the likeness of sinful flesh." Rom. 8:3

"As we have borne the image of the earthy, we shall also bear the image of the heavenly."

I Cor. 15:49

Every man, they say, has his double. Sometimes that strikes us as strange, and yet, on second thought, it isn't so strange at all. The human population of the earth stands somewhere in the region of 2,900,000,-000 persons. Each of them has in front of his head a small patch of skin measuring some six inches by four, whose topography (apart from variations due to race, sex and age) is all pretty much the same. Surely it should scarcely seem odd to us if, among all those, some are so much alike as to be "the image" of another.

Here are four images:

1. The image of the creature
   "And God said, Let us make man in our own image, after our likeness."
2. The image of the sinner
   "And Adam . . . begat a son in his own likeness, after his image."
3. The image of the Saviour
   "[Christ] who is the image of the invisible God."
   "God sending his own Son in the likeness of sinful flesh."
4. The image of the saint
   "As we have borne the image of the earthy, so shall we bear the image of the heavenly."

7. MAN IN THE IMAGE OF GOD

"So God created man in his own image, in the image of God created he him."   GEN. 1:27

It must never be forgotten that all truth lies in the order of life itself. There is a natural environment and in it have been, real and mighty from the beginning, the laws and forces which science has but recently discovered.

Notice:

1. If man had understood himself, he would have seen in himself the interpreter of nature.

2. Religion is the interpreter of man.
3. Christianity is the interpreter of religion.
4. God is the interpreter of Christianity.

—George A. Gordon

8. THE THREE BREATHINGS OF GOD

1. God breathes into man the breath of physical life.

"The Lord God . . . breathed into his nostrils the breath of life." Gen. 2:7

2. God breathes into man the breath of intellectual life.

"The spirit of God hath made me, and the breath of the Almighty hath given me life."
Job 33:4

3. God breathes into man the breath of spiritual life.

"He breathed on them, and saith unto them, Receive ye the Holy Ghost." John 20:22

9. THE FOUR HEARTS OF WOMAN

"She shall be called, Woman, because she was taken out of Man." GEN. 2:23

Every woman has four hearts:

1. The heart of a child
2. The heart of a sister
3. The heart of a bride
4. The heart of a mother

—Unknown

10. THE SERPENT AS A SYMBOL FOR SIN

"Now the serpent was more subtil than any beast of the field which the Lord God had made."

GEN. 3:1

Why is the serpent a suitable symbol for sin? I suggest three reasons.

1. Because of its mesmerism

In its tiny beady eyes it has bewitching power, casting a spell over its prey. So does sin.

2. Because of its subtlety
   The lion leaps on its victim with a growl, the snake glides up to it surreptitiously. So does sin. .

3. Because of the fatal nature of its poisoning
   The venom of some reptiles is so deadly that when one has been injected with it only twenty minutes of life remain. So with sin.

11. THE VOICE OF THE DEVIL

"The serpent," it has been said, "is the eternal question mark." It is significant that on each of the occasions here listed on which we hear the accents of Satan in the Bible his utterance is consonant with his character. He is the embodiment of interrogation.

1. "Yea, hath God said?" Gen. 3:1
2. "Doth Job fear God for nought?" Job 1:9
3. "If thou be the Son of God." Matt. 4:3

—George Campbell Morgan

12. THE GARDEN OF THE LORD

"And Adam and his wife hid themselves from the presence of the Lord God among the trees of the garden." GEN. 3:8

The garden of the Lord concealed from Adam and Eve the Lord of the garden.

1. One of the trees behind which the face of the Lord becomes hidden from us is the tree of knowledge.
2. Another tree behind which the face of the Lord becomes hidden from us is that of material prosperity.
3. One more tree behind which the face of the Lord becomes hidden from us is that of moral respectability.

—Charles H. Parkhurst, Three Gates on a Side

13. A DIVINE INQUIRY

"Where art thou?" GEN. 3:9
1. Everybody is somewhere.

    2. Some folks are where they have no business to be.

    3. No one is where God cannot find him.

—Thomas Champness

14. THREE SEARCHING DEMANDS

    1. "Where art thou?" Gen. 3:9

    2. "Where is Abel thy brother?" Gen. 4:9

    3. "Where is the lamb?" Gen. 22:7

15. HIDING FROM GOD

A man may hide God from himself, but he cannot hide himself from God. Yet some try.

    1. The hiding of guilt

        "I was afraid . . . and hid myself."

Gen. 3:10

    2. The hiding of sloth

        "I was afraid, and went and hid thy talent."

Matt. 25:25

    3. The hiding of reverence

        "Moses hid his face; for he was afraid to look upon God." Exod. 3:6

16. POPULAR EXCUSES FOR SIN

"And the man said, The woman whom thou gavest to be with me, she gave me of the tree, and I did eat. And the Lord God said unto the woman, What is this that thou hast done? And the woman said, The serpent beguiled me, and I did eat."

Gen. 3:12-13

Consider some popular excuses for sin:

    1. There is no harm in it.

    2. Others do it.

    3. I must live.

    4. My motive is good.

—John A. Kern,
The Ministry to the Congregation

17. THE GUARDED GATE

"So he drove out the man; and he placed at the east of the garden of Eden Cherubims, and a flam-

ing sword which turned every way, to keep the way
of the tree of life." GEN. 3:24

1. God is always driving us out of our Edens
   when by sin we have unfitted ourselves for
   staying in them.
2. Angels guarded the gate—not devils. It is a
   mercy sinful man cannot get back into Paradise Lost.
3. When man left Eden, he took the vision of
   it with him—the ideal could never wholly
   fade from his imagination.

—James Wright

18. MARKS

"The Lord set a mark upon Cain." GEN. 4:15
"Except I shall see in his hands the print of the
nails . . . I will not believe." JOHN 20:25
"I bear in my body the marks of the Lord Jesus."
GAL. 6:17

Not many of us are sufficiently outstanding to make
our mark in the world, but all of us bear marks of
some kind. Consider the following three sorts of
mark:

1. The mark of the sinner
2. The mark of the Saviour
3. The mark of the saint

19. BRIEF BIOGRAPHY

"He was not; for God took him." GEN. 5:24
The life of every deceased Christian may be
summed up, as might that of Enoch, thus:

1. He was—for God made him.
2. He was not—for God took him.
3. He is—for God has him.

20. THE FOUR HARVESTS OF THE BIBLE

1. The harvest of providence
   "Seedtime and harvest . . . shall not cease."
   Gen. 8:22

2. The harvest of moral consequence
"Whatsoever a man soweth, that shall he also reap." Gal. 6:7

3. The harvest of evangelism
"For they [the fields] are white already to harvest." John 4:35

4. The harvest of the final judgment
"The harvest is the end of the world."
Matt. 13:39

21. THE BOW IN THE CLOUD
"I do set my bow in the cloud." GEN. 9:13

1. What we most dread, God can illuminate.
2. There is an unchanging purpose in the most changing things.
3. There is healing in the mystery of things.
4. The background of joy is sorrow.
5. There is mercy over the portal of God's dwelling.

—G. H. Morrison, *The Incomparable Christ*

22. WHY GOD ALLOWS THE CLOUDS TO COME
"When I bring a cloud." GEN. 9:14

What do clouds bring in human life?

1. Clouds darken life.
No life is without its gloom.
2. Clouds temper life.
They bring shadow as well as showers.
3. Clouds fertilize life.
"All sunshine makes a desert."
4. Clouds beautify life.
Not all clouds are grey and lowering. Some are gilded with the glow of dawn or sunset, or shot through with the brilliant tapestry of a rainbow.

23. HALFWAY HOUSE
"And Terah died in Haran." GEN. 11:32

Many are like Terah. They go only halfway with God.

1. Some only go halfway where the creed is concerned.

   They do not believe all that they ought to believe as Christians.

2. Some only go halfway where conduct is concerned.

   They go one mile with Christ, but refuse to go the second mile.

3. Some only go halfway where the church is concerned.

   They attend it, but they do not actively participate in its work and witness.

   Note: We ought to go all the way.

24. FOUR STEPS IN ABRAM'S LIFE

1. He went forth—separation.

   "Abram . . . went forth to go into the land of Canaan." Gen. 12:5

2. He went down—decline.

   "And Abram went down into Egypt."
   Gen. 12:10

3. He went up—restoration.

   "And Abram went up out of Egypt."
   Gen. 13:1

4. He went on—progress.

   "And Abram moved his tent, and came and dwelt by the oaks of Mamre."
   Gen. 13:18
   —Unknown

25. AMENING GOD

"*Abram amened Jehovah, and it was imputed unto him for righteousness.*" Gen. 15:6

1. We ought to say "Amen" to God's plan for our spiritual recovery.

2. We ought to say "Amen" to God's providential dealings in our life.

3. We ought to say "Amen" to God's programme for our age.

19

26. QUO VADIS?

(A New Year Sermon outline)

"Hagar, Sarai's maid, whence camest thou? and whither wilt thou go?" GEN. 16:8

In the light of that query, "Whither wilt thou go?" let us consider our whereabouts and our direction.

1. Look at the words from the physical point of view. Whither are we tending in bodily health?
2. Look at the words from the moral point of view. Whither are we tending in character?
3. Look at the words from the spiritual and religious point of view. Whither are we tending in the life of the Spirit?

—D. C. Mitchell, *The Nonsense of Neutrality*

27. GOD LOOKING ON HUMAN SUFFERING

"Thou God seest me." GEN. 16:13

The higher the rank and positions of men, the more difficult it is for common people to have their attention. But God, who is the highest and greatest of all, is equally approachable by everyone. "Thou God seest me." Who said that? Not a king, not a potentate, not a prophet, but a fugitive slave girl in the desert.

On the evidence of this ancient story, what sort of look shall we say God bestows on human suffering?

1. It is a penetrating look.
    Hagar felt that God's eye looked through her, saw every thought, sentiment, feeling. "Thou God seest me"—not my dress, my poverty, my sin, but me.
2. It is a pitying look.
    "The angel of the Lord found her by a fountain of water in the wilderness."
    (vs. 7)
3. It is a pointing look.
    "Return to thy mistress, and submit thyself under her hands." (vs. 9)
    Adapted.

    —Z. Mather, *The Christ of the Heart*

28. THE ALL-SEEING GOD

"Thou God seest me." GEN. 16:13

Think of:

1. The wonder of it

> "God," declared Robert Boyle, "beholds at once all that every one of His creatures, whether visible or invisible to us, in the vast universe, either does or thinks."

2. The challenge of it

> There was in ancient times a form of punishment which consisted in placing the prisoner in a narrow cell in the door of which was a small aperture. At that aperture there was always a warder's eye. What a challenge that constant and unremitting invigilation must have been!

3. The comfort of it

> It is not a stern warder who is watching us: it is a loving Father.

29. SPIRITUAL PROGRESS

"Walk before me, and be thou perfect."
GEN. 17:1

"Walk after the Lord your God." DEUT. 13:4

"Enoch walked with God." GEN. 5:24

A preposition, it has been said, will sometimes greatly modify the meaning of a proposition. Note the prepositions here:

1. Walk before God—that is the walk of duty.
2. Walk after God—that is the walk of discipleship.
3. Walk with God—that is the walk of devotion.

30. THE ENOUGH

"I am the Almighty God." (*El Shaddai*)
GEN. 17:1

The term is not adequate, I know. It falls very far short of the facts. But, as a working equivalent of *El Shaddai*, the great Hebrew name for God, I do not think it could be bettered. "The Enough!"

Of many things in the world men feel they have not enough—money, power, learning, and so on. It is an illusion. An old Welsh proverb reminds us of the reality. "Without God, without anything. God—and enough."

Let us try to think of one or two senses in which God is the Enough.

1. He is the Enough in creation.

There was no absolute need, so far as we can see, to build the universe on so colossal a scale. Its vastness is eloquent of the fact that God is the Enough.

2. He is the Enough in providence.

That seems a daring claim to make in face of the famished millions of the Far East. Yet any economist will tell you that they are starving today not because of a failure of world supply but because of a failure in distribution.

3. He is the Enough in grace.

"Its streams the whole creation reach,
      So plenteous is its store;
  Enough for all, enough for each,
      Enough for evermore."

—Charles Wesley

31. CRYSTALLIZING RETROSPECT

"But his wife looked back from behind him, and she became a pillar of salt." GEN. 19:26

It is very little we know of this woman. We do not even know her name. Yet Jesus bids us remember her, not to imitate her but to take warning from her tragic folly. Note:

1. She was lost in the best connections.
   Wife of "righteous Lot."
2. She was lost in the best company.
   Angels had been her guests.
3. She was lost on the best way.
   She was heading for safety when she turned back.
4. She was lost in consequence of what seems a very trifling thing.

She did not go back, she merely looked back.

—W. Price

32. THE DESERT, THE CUP AND THE WELL

"And God opened her eyes, and she saw a well of water." GEN. 21:19

In the story of Abraham this event reveals a mixture of fulfillment and sorrow, blessing and tragedy. The son, hitherto favored, becomes an outcaste. From this picture of the fugitive mother and her son, we take three things to remember:

1. The way of loss and hardship may help us to discover God's purpose for us.
2. How much sometimes depends on so little!
3. There is so much we never see until God gives us sight.

—Unknown

33. HUMAN OFFERINGS OF THE BIBLE

GEN. 22:1-19; JUDG. 11:29-40; JOHN 3:16

1. The sacrifice that need not be made—
   Abraham offering Isaac.
2. The sacrifice that should never have been made—
   Jephthah offering his daughter.
3. The sacrifice that had to be made—
   God offering his Son.

34. THE LAMB

1. The cry of the Old Testament
   "Where is the lamb?" Gen. 22:7
2. The cry of the New Testament
   "Behold the Lamb." John 1:29
3. The cry of heaven
   "Worthy is the Lamb." Rev. 5:12

35. DEALING FAIRLY WITH GOD

"And now if ye will deal kindly and truly with my master, tell me: and if not, tell me; that I may *turn to the right hand, or to the left."*

GEN. 24:49

There are certain paramount reasons why we should deal fairly with God.

1. Because of what he is
2. Because of what he has done
3. Because of what he will do

—J. Wilbur Chapman, *Another Mile*

36. THE THREE NAMES OF JACOB

"His name was called Jacob." GEN. 25:26
"I am Esau." GEN. 27:19
"Thy name shall be called no more Jacob, but Israel." GEN. 32:28

1. There is the name his parents gave him. "Jacob"
2. There is the name he gave himself. "Esau"
3. There is the name God gave him. "Israel"

37. THE BARTERED BIRTHRIGHT

GEN. 25:27-34
HEB. 12:16-17

Four points protrude from this familiar narrative:

1. The clamorous demands of the physical
   "Jacob sod pottage: and Esau came from the field, and he was faint: and Esau said to Jacob, Feed me, I pray thee."

   Gen. 25:29-30

2. The seeming unreality of the spiritual
   "What profit shall this birthright do to me?" Gen. 25:32
3. The inevitability of choice
   "Sell me this day." Gen. 25:31
4. The permanent impoverishment which results from the wrong decision.
   "Lest there be any fornicator, or profane person, as Esau, who for one morsel of meat sold his birthright. For ye know how that

afterward, when he would have inherited the blessing, he was rejected: for he found no place of repentance, though he sought it carefully with tears." Heb. 12:16-17

38. THE UNDEFINED DEMAND

"Feed me . . . with that same red. . . ."

GEN. 25:30

You will notice that in your King James Version of the Bible the term "pottage" is in italics. This means, as you know, that it does not occur in the original, but was inserted by the translators in the interest of clarity. Significantly, Esau halts without naming the dish on which he yearns to dine.

I wonder why.

1. Perhaps it was haste that caused Esau thus to break off abruptly.
2. Perhaps it was ignorance which brought him to this sudden stop. He who would fain partake of sin's fare does not know what he is asking for.
3. Perhaps it was contempt which accounted for his declinature to name the dish.

39. THE CHOKED WELLS

"And Isaac digged again the wells of water, which they had digged in the days of Abraham his father."

GEN. 26:18

1. The wells of our fathers may get choked.
2. We must each dig for ourselves to reach the water.
3. Our rediscovered wells were named long since.

—G. H. Morrison, *The Incomparable Christ*

40. HOW WELLS RUN DRY

"And Isaac digged again the wells of water, which they had digged in the days of Abraham his father; for the Philistines had stopped them after the death of Abraham: and he called their names after the names by which his father had called them."

GEN. 26:18

1. Wells sometimes run dry because they are neglected.
2. Wells sometimes run dry because of subterranean change.
3. Wells sometimes run dry because of the behavior of passers-by.

—John A. Hutton

41. REOPENING THE OLD WELLS

"And Isaac digged again the wells of water, which they had digged in the days of Abraham his father; for the Philistines had stopped them after the death of Abraham; and he called their names after the names by which his father had called them."

GEN. 26:18

1. Isaac reopening the wells is an illustration of the fact that nature is on the side of the man who tries to do good. Isaac had to dig the wells, but if God had not sent the water he would have dug in vain.
2. Isaac reopening the wells is an illustration of the truth that one man is often called upon to revive or to complete the work of another.
3. Isaac reopening the wells is an illustration of how anyone attempting such a task has to remove the hindrances caused by evil men.
4. Isaac reopening the wells is an illustration of how one person can be the means of bringing great blessing to many.

—H. C. Williams, *Christ the Centre*

42. GOD—MAKING ROOM FOR US

"The Lord hath made room for us."

GEN. 26:22

1. God has made ample room for us in nature. It is said that the entire population of the world could stand on the Isle of Wight. But we are not thus cramped together. God has provided a spacious universe for us to dwell in.

2. God has made ample room for us in grace. "Yet there is room." Luke 14:22
3. God has made ample room for us in heaven. "In my Father's house are many mansions: if it were not so, I would have told you." John 14:2

43. THREE-DIMENSIONAL LIVING

"And he [Isaac] builded an altar there, and called upon the name of the Lord, and pitched his tent there: and there Isaac's servants digged a well." GEN. 26:25

Here is life in three dimensions:
1. Life's upward reference
   "He builded an altar."
2. Life's outward relationships
   "[He] pitched his tent."
3. Life's deep resources
   "There Isaac's servants digged a well."

44. ESCAPISM

It is perfectly legitimate, indeed it is instinctive, to seek to escape from danger; but escapism may be defined as a desire to escape from something from which we should not try to escape.
Escapism is a prevalent modern mental attitude. To what is it to be traced?
1. It may be guilt that makes us escapists.
   Jacob fleeing from Esau: Gen. 27:41-45
2. It may be discouragement that makes us escapists.
   Elijah fleeing from Jezebel: I Kings 19:1-8
3. It may be self-will that makes us escapists.
   Jonah fleeing from God: Jonah 1:1-3
4. It is basically fear that makes us escapists.
   The disciples fleeing from the Temple guard: Mark 14:43-50

45. WHEN GOD BECOMES REAL

"And he lighted upon a certain place, and tarried there all night, because the sun was set; . . . And

27

he dreamed, and behold a ladder set up on the earth, and the top of it reached to heaven. . . . And, behold, the Lord stood above it."

GEN. 28:11-13

1. Jacob at Bethel was in the right place for a vital experience of God:
    In a wilderness, alone, at the end of the day.
2. Jacob at Bethel was lying on the right kind of pillow:
    The hard stones of that bleak hillside.
3. Jacob at Bethel was in the right mood:
    He was a fugitive from the wrath of a wronged brother, burdened doubtless with a sense of shame.

—G. T. Bellhouse, Our Sufficient Beauty

46. THE LADDER OF PRAYER

"Behold a ladder set up on the earth, and the top of it reached to heaven." GEN. 28:12
The ladder of prayer has four rungs:

1. The first rung—prayer as a cry of escape from some external evil.
2. The second rung—prayer as a cry for deliverance from sin.
3. The third rung—prayer for virtue and needed grace.
4. The fourth rung—prayer as a merging of our wills in the will of God.

—G. H. Morrison, The Incomparable Christ

47. THE LAD AND THE LADDER

"And he dreamed, and behold a ladder set up on the earth, and the top of it reached to heaven."

GEN. 28:12

Four things about a ladder call for special mention:

1. A ladder is a short thing.
    Heaven is nearer than we think.

2. A ladder is a straight thing.
   If not straight it is not safe.
3. A ladder is a narrow thing.
   Only room for us to go up, as the Irishman said, "one abreast."
4. A ladder is a portable thing.
   It can be taken away. Hence the urgent need to start climbing to heaven today.

48. THREE SCENES IN THE LIFE OF JACOB

There are three clearly defined stages in the religious development of Jacob.

1. Jacob dreaming
   "And he dreamed, and behold a ladder set up on the earth, and the top of it reached to heaven."   Gen. 28:12
2. Jacob wrestling
   "And Jacob was left alone; and there wrestled a man with him until the breaking of the day."   Gen. 32:24
3. Jacob blessing
   "All these are the twelve tribes of Israel: and this is it that their father spake unto them, and blessed them; every one according to his blessing he blessed them."
   Gen. 49:28

49. THREE SURPRISES IN JACOB'S DREAM

And [Jacob] dreamed, and behold a ladder set up on the earth, and the top of it reached to heaven: and behold the angels of God ascending and descending on it. And, behold, the Lord stood above it, and said, I am the Lord God of Abraham thy father, and the God of Isaac.   GEN. 28:12-13

It might not be wise for the preacher to claim that each occurrence in the Bible of the word "behold" must be taken to imply an element of surprise.

Here, however, we do feel that surprise is expressed.

1. There is the surprise of the shining stairway. "Behold a ladder."

2. There is the surprise of the celestial traffic. "Behold the angels of God."

3. There is the surprise of the revealing God. "Behold, the Lord."

—Harold T. Barrow

50. UNEXPECTED REVELATIONS OF GOD

"And Jacob awaked out of his sleep, and he said, Surely the Lord is in this place; and I knew it not." GEN. 28:16

1. God sometimes reveals himself unexpectedly in the realm of nature.

2. God sometimes reveals himself unexpectedly amid the ordinary surroundings of life.

3. God sometimes reveals himself unexpectedly in the hour of loneliness and trial.

4. God sometimes reveals himself unexpectedly in the hour of spiritual abasement.

—John C. Lambert

51. WAGES

"What shall thy wages be?" GEN. 29:15

1. The wages of domestic duty. "Take this child away, and nurse it for me, and I will give thee thy wages."

Exod. 2:9

2. The wages of evangelistic activity. "He that reapeth receiveth wages."

John 4:36

3. The wages of immorality. "The wages of sin is death."

Rom. 6:23

52. LEARNING BY EXPERIENCE

"I have learned by experience." GEN. 30:27

1. Experience is a great teacher.

2. Her fees are often high.

3. We grudge the cost of the tuition.

4. In the end we perceive that the education has been worth the expense.

53. MIDNIGHT CRISIS

GEN. 32:24-32

Three words sum up the story of Jacob's encounter with the angel and its effect upon his character.

1. Crooked
2. Crippled
3. Crowned

54. JACOB AT JABBOK

"And Jacob was left alone; and there wrestled a man with him until the breaking of the day."

GEN. 32:24

Four lessons may be learned from this story.

1. He who would walk in the light must first wrestle in the dark.
2. He who would have his name and nature changed for the better must first learn the name and the nature of God.
3. He who would win must first suffer himself to be overcome.

    "He does not mean to wrestle all night for nothing." (Matthew Henry)

    "Jacob was knighted on the field." (Thomas Scott)
4. He who would clasp his wronged brother must first come to grips with God.

55. WRESTLING JACOB

"And Jacob was left alone; and there wrestled a man with him until the breaking of the day."

GEN. 32:24

We have here a striking illustration of the truth that:

1. There is deep loneliness in all real distress.
2. In this loneliness the only effective resource is the Lord himself.
3. Though our first advances to the Lord may seem to be repulsed, perseverance will at last prevail.
4. Such an experience leaves its mark on the one

who has passed through it and makes memorable the place where it was undergone.

—W. M. Taylor, *The Limitations of Life*

56. ON SEEING GOD IN THE FACE OF MAN

"And Jacob said, Nay, I pray thee, if now I have found grace in thy sight, then receive my present at my hand: for therefore I have seen thy face, as though I had seen the face of God, and thou wast pleased with me."

GEN. 33:10

Man becomes Godlike when he forgives. That is the teaching of the text. Blessed be those who, when we have wronged them but have sought for reconciliation, by their attitude toward us make real to us the forgiveness of God.

How did Esau, in thus exercising the royal prerogative of pardon, become like God?

1. He became like God by extending grace to the offender.

   "If now I have found grace in thy sight."

2. He became like God by making no reference to the repented wrong.

3. He became like God by offering his fellowship and service to the one who, though now truly penitent, had once treated him so shabbily.

   "And he said, Let us take our journey, and let us go, and I will go before thee"—as guide and protector. Gen. 33:12

57. SEEING GOD IN ESAU

"I have seen thy face, as though I had seen the face of God." GEN. 33:10.

Jacob saw God in Esau. That, to anyone who knows the history of their respective characters and mutual relations, is simply staggering. Had Esau seen God in Jacob that would have been surprising enough, but that Jacob should have seen God in Esau seems dead against all the probabilities.

Yet so it was. And we may see God in our Esaus. For note:

1. We cannot clearly see the face of God, if the face of some wronged Esau come between.
2. We can only see the face of God in Esau's when we endeavor, so far as lies in our power, to put right the wrong relationship between us.
3. It is the duty of those who have been wronged and of whom the offender begs forgiveness, to mediate and make real to the penitent the redeeming mercy of God.

58. THE COMING OF THE DREAMER

"Behold, this dreamer cometh." GEN. 37:19

I take two points:

1. The dreamer

There are four outstanding characteristics of the dreamer that I want to press upon your consideration.

   a) He had the eye of a seer.
   b) He had the faith of a prophet.
   c) He had the heart of a brother.
   d) He had the courage of a warrior.

2. The dream

What did the dream do for Joseph?

   a) It gave direction to his life.
   b) It delivered him in the hour of temptation.
   c) It comforted him in the hour of his sorest trial.
   d) It crowned him with enduring glory.

   —W. W. Weeks, *The Face of Christ*

59. A LUCKY FELLOW

"The Lord was with Joseph, and he was a prosperous man." GEN. 39:2

There is a very vivid and colorful version of this text in Tyndale's translation of the Old Testament. "The Lord was with Joseph, and he was a lucky fellow."

Why was Joseph a lucky fellow?

1. Because of his integrity

2. Because of his industry
3. Because of his fidelity
4. Because of his magnanimity

60. MAN OF ACTION

"Whatsoever they did there, he was the doer of it." GEN. 39:22

1. Such a man multiplies his own powers by putting purpose into others.
2. Such a man expands the possibilities of others by inspiring them to do what, without him, they would never have attempted.
3. Such a man gets things done in the world by setting his will to work in regions beyond the direct reach of his personality.
4. Such a man gets the credit for things he could never have accomplished without the aid of lesser men.

61. IS THE UNIVERSE FRIENDLY?

F. W. H. Myers was once asked: "If you could put one question only to the Sphinx and were sure of getting a reply, what would the question be?" He thought for a moment and then made answer. "My question would be: Is the universe friendly?"
Here are three biblical statements that bear directly on that subject.

1. The universe is inimical.
   "All these things are against me."
   Gen. 42:36
2. The universe is indifferent.
   "All things continue as they were."
   II Pet. 3:4
3. The universe is co-operative.
   "All things work together for good."
   Rom. 8:28
   This last judgment can be justly made only by Christians.

62. THE CONQUEST OF THE CUP

"Put my cup, the silver cup, in the sack's mouth of the youngest." GEN. 44:2

1. The commitment of the cup
2. The communion of the cup
3. The conquest of the cup
—Hubert L. Simpson, *Communion Addresses*

63. FORGET IT

"*Regard not your stuff.*" GEN. 45:20

1. That would divide your mind.
2. That would weaken your resolve.
3. That might debase your character.

64. THE WITNESS OF THE WAGONS

"*It is enough; Joseph my son is yet alive: I will go and see him.*" GEN. 45:28

Jacob did not believe that Joseph, his beloved son whom he had supposed dead, was alive—until he saw the wagons. They convinced him that the tale was true.

People do not believe that Jesus is alive. Are there any things in the world today corresponding to the wagons in this story, calculated to persuade men of the credibility of the report of Christ's resurrection? There are!

1. The Church is such a wagon.

   It simply could not have existed unless Christ had risen from the grave.
2. The New Testament is such a wagon.

   If Jesus had not triumphed over the tomb the Christian scriptures would never have been penned.
3. Sunday is such a wagon.

   Were Christ still in the sepulchre, the first day of the week would never have been observed as a holiday throughout the Christian world.

65. THE LION OF JUDAH

"*The scepter shall not depart from Judah,
    nor the ruler's staff from between his feet,
until he comes to whom it belongs;*

35

and to him shall be the obedience of the
peoples." GEN. 49:10 R.S.V.

How were these words concerning Judah fulfilled?

1. The tribe of Judah soon rose into leadership.
   It was the largest of the tribes that left
   Egypt. In the wilderness, when the twelve
   tribes were divided into four camps, Judah
   was given the eastern position toward the
   rising of the sun. The tribe of Judah led the
   march toward Canaan.

2. David, the great king, belonged to the tribe
   of Judah.

3. Matthew traces the human ancestry of our
   Lord and Saviour Jesus Christ to the same
   tribe (Matt. 1:17). "It is evident that our
   Lord sprang out of Juda." (Heb. 7:14)

   —J. Allan Wright

66. THE WALL, THE WELL, THE WINE

"Joseph is a fruitful bough, even a fruitful bough by
a well; whose branches run over the wall."

GEN. 49:22

1. Every life does have its walls.
2. Every life should have its well.
3. Every life can have its wine.

EXODUS

67. POSTNATAL CARE

"Take this child away, and nurse it for me, and I
will give thee thy wages." EXOD. 2:9

Consider:

1. The nurse
2. The child

3. The wages

—T. Harwood Pattison,
The Making of a Sermon

68. THREE EPOCHS IN THE LIFE OF MOSES

1. Forty years thinking he was somebody
   "The child grew, and she brought him unto Pharaoh's daughter, and he became her son." Exod. 2:10
2. Forty years learning he was nobody
   "Moses fled from the face of Pharaoh, and dwelt in the land of Midian." Exod. 2:15
3. Forty years finding that God was everybody
   "Consider that this nation is thy people."
   Exod. 33:13

—Unknown

69. THREE EPOCHS IN THE LIFE OF MOSES

1. A period of self-aggrandizement
   Exod. 2:10
2. A period of self-abasement   Exod. 2:15
3. A period of self-commitment   Exod. 33:13

70. THE CALL OF MOSES
Exod. 3:1-11

1. The sight that made him stop
   "I will now turn aside, and see this great sight." (vs. 3)
2. The step that made him great
   "He turned aside to see." (vs. 4)
   He saw the great sight and the great sight made him a great man.
3. The sound that made him bow
   "Moses, Moses"! (vs. 4)
4. The summons that made him act
   "Come now therefore, and I will send thee." (vs. 10)

—David Hogg

71. GOD AS FIRE

"*The angel of the Lord appeared unto him* [Moses] *in a flame of fire.*" Exod. 3:2

1. Fire consumes
2. Fire purifies
3. Fire breaks
4. Fire softens
5. Fire hardens
6. Fire inflames
7. Fire warms
8. Fire cheers
9. Fire fuses
10. Fire assimilates
11. Fire tests
12. Fire illuminates
13. Fire moves
14. Fire ascends

—F. E. Marsh, *Emblems of the Holy Spirit*

72. THE BURNING BUSH

"*And the angel of the Lord appeared to him* [Moses] *in a flame of fire out of the midst of a bush.*" Exod. 3:2

1. It was a flaming tree.
2. It was an indestructible tree.
3. It was a speaking tree.

Apply this to the Cross.

73. THE BURNING BUSH

"*And Moses said, I will now turn aside, and see this great sight, why the bush is not burnt.*"

Exod. 3:3

Nothing reveals a person more than the nature of the things he turns aside to see. As children we turned aside to see the toy shops; later we turned aside to look into the windows of jewellers' establishments; later still we turned aside to examine the products of furniture manufacturers; and after a while we were back at the toy shops again! Each was a revelation of our character and interests.

Note here:
1. Some see only the bush
2. Some see also the burning
3. Some see the Being
   "Moses hid his face; for he was afraid to look upon God."

74. ARE YOU THERE?

"Here am I." Exod. 3:4; I Sam. 3:4; Isa. 6:8
1. God calls in nature.
   Moses heard the divine summons there and responded: "Here am I."
2. God calls in the human heart.
   Samuel heard the divine summons there and responded: "Here am I."
3. God calls in the sanctuary.
   Isaiah heard the divine summons there and responded: "Here am I."

75. GOD INTRODUCING HIMSELF

"I am the God of thy father, the God of Abraham, the God of Isaac, and the God of Jacob."

Exod. 3:6

The text implies:
1. That God is the God of succeeding generations.
2. That God is the God of differing personalities.
3. That God is the God of individual beings.

—William Davies

76. THE ESSENCE ALL-DIVINE

"And God said unto Moses, I am that I am; and he said, Thus shalt thou say unto the children of Israel, I am hath sent me unto you."

Exod. 3:14

Although God is omnipotent, omniscient and omnipresent, in the light of the Cross it is seen that:
1. God's omnipotence is not a force that crushes, but love equal to all the demands made upon it.

39

2. God's omniscience means that the God who saves knows all about us.
3. God's omnipresence means that we cannot drift beyond his love and care.
    —Alwyn Lake Thomas, *Things that Matter*

77. WHY THEY SAID IT

"*I have sinned.*" Exod. 10:16; I Sam. 15:30; Matt. 27:3-4; Luke 15:21

Burns speaks of "the moving why." To grasp what men intend to convey you must not only listen to what they say but ask why they say it. Motive modifies meaning and may even make all the difference in the issue between life and death.

Note why the four biblical characters named in our texts uttered this confession.
1. Pharaoh uttered it in fear of retribution.
2. Saul made it in dread of exposure.
3. Judas voiced it in hopeless remorse.
4. The Prodigal expressed it in genuine repentance.

78. THE DIFFERENCE BETWEEN THEM

"*But all the children of Israel had light in their dwellings.*" Exod. 10:23
1. There should always be a notable difference between God's people and others.
2. That difference, where it exists, is due to the fact that God's people possess light unknown to others.
3. The difference is designed not so much to condemn as to challenge.

79. COMPROMISES

"*Our cattle also shall go with us; there shall not an hoof be left behind.*" Exod. 10:26
Let us consider the four compromises Pharaoh suggested to Moses and then the answer of consecration to them all.

1. Compromises suggested
   a) "Don't go: worship your God in Egypt."
   b) "Go, but don't go very far away."
   c) "Let the men go, but leave the women and the little ones."
   d) "Go and take your families with you, but don't take your cattle."
2. The answer of consecration
   a) Complete defiance of Pharaoh.
   b) Refusal to leave anything in the land that might later be used by the enemy.
   c) Insistence that the cattle go along with them because they would be needed for sacrifice in the wilderness.

   —W. W. Weeks, *The Face of Christ*

80. THE MEANING OF THE SACRAMENT

"*What mean ye by this service?*"   Exod. 12:26

1. It means commemoration.
2. It means communion.
3. It means commitment.
4. It means consecration.

—Murdo Ewen Macdonald,
The Vitality of Faith

81. THE ROUNDABOUT ROUTE

"*God led them not through the way of the land of the Philistines, although that was near. . . . God led the people about.*"   Exod. 13:17-18
"*And he led them forth by the right way.*"
Ps. 107:7

The roundabout way was the right way. Why?

1. Short cuts are often longest.
2. Long routes are sometimes safest.
3. On the roundabout route you see the most.

82. COUNSEL IN A CRISIS

1. The people said: "Go back."
   "Because there were no graves in Egypt, hast thou taken us away to die in the wilderness?"

. . . It had been better for us to serve the Egyptians, than that we should die in the wilderness." Exod. 14:11-12
2. Moses said: "Stand still."
"Stand still, and see the salvation of the Lord." Exod. 14:13
3. God said: "Go forward."
"Speak unto the children of Israel, that they go forward." Exod. 14:15

—W. E. Sangster,
The Craft of Sermon Construction

83. GOD—PROHIBITING PRAYER

"And the Lord said unto Moses, Wherefore criest thou unto me?" Exod. 14:15

This is one of the strangest and most staggering texts in the Bible. In it we find God actually forbidding a man to pray. That is not like God. Always he is bidding men to pray, but here forbidding. Why?

1. It is impertinent to pray for God to do anything until you yourself have done all you can.
"Speak . . . lift up thy rod."
Exod. 14:15-17
2. It is impertinent to pray when God has already given you clear guidance which you have not obeyed.
3. It is impertinent to pray for God to act before his time to act has come.

84. GOD'S GLORY IN THE MORNING

"And in the morning, then ye shall see the glory of the Lord." Exod. 16:7

Let us take these lovely words of hope and promise out of their historic framework in the record of Israel's deliverance from Egypt, and let us seek to read their message for ourselves.

Let us take it:

1. For every new day that comes to us.
2. For the Lord's day in particular.
3. For the morning of life.

4. For seasons of religious quickening and revival.
5. For the restoring of the soul.

—James S. Stewart, *The Strong Name*

85. MOSES ON THE MOUNTS

"The Lord called Moses up to the top of the mount; and Moses went up." Exod. 19:20

"And Moses went up from the plains of Moab unto the mountain of Nebo." Deut. 34:1

"And after six days Jesus taketh Peter, James, and John his brother, and bringeth them up into an high mountain apart, And was transfigured before them: and his face did shine as the sun, and his raiment was white as the light. And, behold, there appeared unto them Moses and Elias."

Matt. 17:1-3

What did Moses see on those mountains?

1. On Mount Sinai Moses saw the law.
2. On Mount Nebo Moses saw the land.
3. On Mount Hermon Moses saw the Lord.

86. SERVITUDE OR SERVICE

"And he shall serve him for ever." Exod. 21:6

About this text Frances Ridley Havergal wrote: "A promise only differenced from a threat by one thing—love!" But what a difference that makes!

1. Love makes labor light.
2. Love makes labor efficient.
3. Love makes labor personally enriching.
4. Love makes labor meaningful.

87. THE VISION OF GOD

"They saw God, and did eat and drink."

Exod. 24:11

1. Some eat and drink without seeing God.
2. Some see God, but cannot eat or drink.
3. Some, like those here described, see God and do eat and drink.

—William M. Taylor, *Limitations of Life*

88. OIL

"Oil for the light." Exod. 25:6

Oil has various uses.

1. It is an illuminant.
2. It is a lubricant.
3. It is a medicament.

89 HOLY—BUT STAINED

"Aaron may bear the iniquity of the holy things."
Exod. 28:38

What an odd phrase! "The iniquity of the holy things." Are we guilty of such iniquity? I think we are.

1. There is our penitence
   Is there iniquity in that?
2. There is our worship.
   Is there iniquity in that?
3. There are our prayers.
   Is there iniquity in them?
4. There is our service.
   Is there iniquity in that?
5. There is our giving.
   Is there iniquity in that?

—W. E. Sangster,
Westminster Sermons (Vol. 1)

90. THE LAW

"And he gave unto Moses, when he had made an end of communing with him upon mount Sinai, two tables of testimony, tables of stone, written with the finger of God." Exod. 31:18

What is the law?

1. It is a standard to measure our defects.
2. It is a sword to pierce our conscience.
3. It is a seal to certify that we are in the way of grace.

—F. A. C. Tholuck

91. WHO IS ON THE LORD'S SIDE?

"Then Moses stood in the gate of the camp, and said, Who is on the Lord's side? let him come

unto me." EXOD. 32:26

1. There are two sides.
   a) You can see that in the world.
   b) You can see it in families.
   c) You can see it in your own soul.
2. There are only two sides.
   "Truth forever on the scaffold, Wrong forever on the throne." (James Russell Lowell)
3. A man must be on one side or the other.
   You may remember how a deputation came once to Abraham Lincoln, declaring: "We trust, sir, that God is on our side." To which the president replied: "It is more important for you to make sure that you are on God's side."

   Sings F. W. Faber:
   He always wins who sides with God;
   To him no chance is lost;
   God's will is sweetest to him when
   It triumphs at his cost.

92. GOING FORWARD WITH GOD'S FACE

"My face shall go with thee."
EXOD. 33:14 Young's Literal Translation

There was a little girl who said that what Jesus did by coming to earth was to "put a face on God." What does the promise of our text imply? What does a face do?

1. It establishes identity.
2. It expresses emotion.
3. It exhibits character.
4. It indicates direction.

93. THE GOAL OF PRAYER

"I beseech thee, show me thy glory."
EXOD. 33:18

"My goal," sings the poet, "is God Himself." That, nothing less, is the objective of true prayer. Analyze this yearning. What is it?

45

1. It is a longing for the permanent behind the passing.
2. It is a longing for the personal behind the mechanical.
3. It is a longing for the perfect behind the imperfect.
4. It is a longing for the spiritual behind the material.

94. THE ESSENTIALS OF WORSHIP

"Set in order the things . . . light the lamps . . . hang up the hanging at the court gate."

Exod. 40:4, 8

Here are three essentials of true worship:

1. Order

"Set in order the things." God loves order and liberty. They must always go together. Under that older dispensation order was more in evidence than liberty, for it was more needed at first. Children must be taught order before they are allowed much liberty, and the people of Israel were children in religion.

2. Illumination

"Light the lamps." Order can only come from knowledge of what God desires.

a) Light the lamp of truth.
b) Light the lamp of faith.
c) Light the lamp of hope.
d) Light the lamp of love.

3. Quietude

Order and light are robbed of some of their value if we cannot also get quiet. We must hang up the hanging at the court gate of the mind. Shut out, with God's help, business and social matters. Concentrate on worship.

—Harold T. Barrow

LEVITICUS

95. SALT

"With all thine offerings thou shalt offer salt."
Lev. 2:13

"Salt is a thing on its own," wrote Lionel Fletcher, "a thing without a substitute. You do not compare salt to anything else, but other things must be compared to it. You may say, 'That is salty', but if you say, 'That is salt', you are immediately understood. So Christ desires it to be with His disciples." Consider:

1. The domestic use of salt
   This suggests that the Christian's influence is to be good in his every day living.
2. The medical use of salt
   This speaks of the healing properties which ought to characterize the life of the Christian.
3. The liturgical use of salt
   This intimates that the Christian must ever be on the altar. His life must be marked by devotion and service.

96. THE DEATHLESS FLAME

"And the fire upon the altar shall be burning in it; it shall not be put out." Lev. 6:12

You may have seen the undying fire at the base of the Arc de Triomphe in Paris or the flare of the quenchless flame at the War Memorial in Melbourne. The fire on the Hebrew altar was like that—an unexpiring blaze.

So should the fire be on the mean altar of our hearts.

1. The fire of a pure love for God
2. The fire of a passionate longing for holiness
3. The fire of a consuming zeal for evangelism

97. PALMS AND WILLOWS

"Ye shall take you on the first day . . . branches
of palm trees . . . and willows of the brook; and
ye shall rejoice before the Lord your God seven
days." LEV. 23:40

The palm stands upright in the sun: the willow
droops and weeps. The one is the symbol of gladness, renown, victory, and immortality; the other
of sadness, weakness, humiliation, exile, and death.
Every year the Israelites were to bring both symbols
into the tabernacle, and to rejoice before the Lord.
Let us bring the great teaching of the text home
to ourselves.

> 1. Palm and willow are associated in human life.
>> a) They are to be found in the life of all
>> men.
>> b) They are closely associated in the life
>> of all.
> 2. It is our highest duty and privilege to bring
> both palm and willow before the Lord.
>> a) We must bring both before the Lord
>> in the spirit of thankfulness. "Ye shall
>> rejoice before the Lord your God seven
>> days."
>> b) We must bring both before the Lord
>> that we may find grace to bear them.

—W. L. Watkinson, *The Blind Spot*

NUMBERS

98. THE PROPHETIC OFFICE

"And Moses said unto him, Enviest thou for my
sake? would God that all the Lord's people were
prophets, and that the Lord would put his Spirit
upon them!" NUM. 11:29

As Joseph Parker put it: "We are all God's clergy, and our priesthood has no standing but in our holiness. Not in our intellectual capacity, not in our technical training, not in our official status, but in the sanctification of the will and of the heart—the total sacrifice of the will to God."

How can we all be prophets?

1. We may all be prophets in our loyalty to the stern ideals of duty.
2. We may all be prophets in the clarity of our spiritual vision.
3. We may all be prophets in the passion of our patriotism.
4. We may all be prophets in the fervor of our prayers.
5. We may all be prophets in the influence for righteousness which we exert upon the community of which we form a part.

—R. Moffat Gautrey, *The Glory of Going On*

99. THE OPTIMISTS

"*We are well able.*"   NUM. 13:30

1. Some say it when their animal spirits are high.
2. Some say it when things are going well for them.
3. Some say it because they fail to take the full measure of the difficulties confronting them.
4. Some say it as an expression of a mood which they cannot maintain.
5. Some say it, in humble trust in God, and then go on to prove that it is true.

100. THE OPTIMISM OF FAITH

"*Let us go up at once, and possess it; for we are well able to overcome it.*"   NUM. 13:30

1. The report
2. The resolve
      "Let us go up."
3. The reliance

49

101. THE KING'S HIGHWAY

*"We will go by the king's high way, we will not
turn to the right hand nor to the left."*

Num. 20:17

1. Here was a highway with a hidden story of
   romance.

   It was the king's highway.
2. Here was a highway fraught with risk.

   It wound its way through territory difficult and dangerous for the children of
   Israel.
3. Here was a highway whose end was rapture.

   This is a road whose end is better than
   itself.

   —Robert Barr, *In Sweet Remembrance*

102. THE FLAG OF HEALING

*"And Moses made a serpent of brass, and set it
upon a pole, and it came to pass, that if a serpent
had bitten any man, when he beheld the serpent
of brass, he lived."* Num. 21:9

*"He [Hezekiah] brake in pieces the brazen serpent
that Moses had made: for unto those days the
children of Israel did burn incense to it: and he
called it Nehushtan."* II Kings 18:4

*"And as Moses lifted up the serpent in the wilder-
ness, even so must the Son of man be lifted up."*

John 3:14

During World War II there was in North Wales
a camp of the Royal Army Medical Corps. Above
it flew a flag bearing the traditional symbol of
the serpent coiled around the pole. A lady living
in the locality told me that once, while the troops
were stationed there, her little daughter was taken
ill. While the child was confined to bed her
mother read to her stories from the Bible. Among
them was this narrative of the lifting up of the
brazen serpent. The tiny invalid was fascinated
by the tale and when it was finished exclaimed:
"I know where that serpent is. It's on the flag-
staff at the camp. Take me there, and I'll get
better." Her mother tried to dissuade her, but it

was of no use. The little one persisted and at last, to humor her, the mother gave in and took her to the camp beneath the flag of healing. They were received very kindly by the commanding officer; and, apologetically, the mother explained the position to him. He diagnosed the child's trouble and treated her, and before long she was quite well again.

There is healing for us all beneath this flag.

1. The symbol
    Num. 21:9
2. The idol
    II Kings 18:4
3. The reality
    John 3:14

103. TOWARD THE SUNRISING

"And they journeyed from Oboth, and pitched at Ijeabarim, in the wilderness which is before Moab, toward the sunrising." NUM. 21:11

1. The setting of the way is the first matter that claims our attention.
    "They journeyed . . . in the wilderness."
2. But now notice the direction of the way.
    "Toward the sunrising."
3. May we add a word about the destination which they reached?
    "He led them forth by the right way."
                                                    Ps. 107:7

—*Scottish Free Church Record*

104. A SPIRIT-FILLED MAN

"And the Lord said unto Moses, Take thee Joshua . . . a man in whom is the spirit." NUM. 27:18

Note:

1. His fearlessness
2. His faithfulness
3. His fitness

—John A. Coleman

51

105. WHAT SIN DOES

1. It finds out.
"Be sure your sin will find you out."
Num. 32:23

2. It keeps out.
"There shall in no wise enter into it any thing that defileth." Rev. 21:27

3. It pays out.
"The wages of sin is death."
Rom. 6:23

—Unknown

106. CONCEALMENT OF SIN NO SECURITY TO THE SINNER

"Be sure your sin will find you out."
Num. 32:23

Secret sin will come to light:

1. By remorse of conscience
2. By the power of natural law
3. By the special working of divine providence
4. By the awful revelations of the day of Judgment

—W. Blaikie

DEUTERONOMY

107. POSSESSING OUR POSSESSIONS

"Behold, the Lord thy God hath set the land before thee: go up and possess it, as the Lord God of thy fathers hath said unto thee; fear not, neither be discouraged." Deut. 1:21

1. The provision of God for his people.
"The Lord thy God hath set the land before thee."

2. The purpose of God for his people.
"Go up and possess it."

3. The promise of God to his people.
"Fear not, neither be discouraged."

—Unknown

108. GOD BEFORE US

"The Lord your God which goeth before you."
DEUT. 1:30

There is such a thing as "prevenient grace," God's grace which precedes us. It operates in many ways.

1. Prevenient grace in our redemption
"The Lamb slain from the foundation of the world." Rev. 13:8
2. Prevenient grace in our conversion
"Before that Philip called thee . . . I saw thee." John 1:48
3. Prevenient grace in providential happenings
"Now therefore be not grieved, nor angry with yourselves, that ye sold me hither: for God did send me before you to preserve life." Gen. 45:5
4. Prevenient grace in our final salvation
"I go to prepare a place for you."

John 14:2
—J. Allan Wright

109. OUT OF THE OLD, INTO THE NEW

(A New Year Sermon Outline)

"He brought us out from thence, that he might bring us in." DEUT. 6:23

God brings us:

1. Out of the old life of sin, into the new life of salvation
2. Out of the old life of last year, into the new life of this year
3. Out of the old life of earth, into the new life of heaven

110. NOT YET COME

(A New Year Sermon Outline)
"Ye are not as yet come." DEUT. 12:9

Moses was at the end of his dealings with the

Israelites, but God was not at the end of his dealings with them. Nor is God yet at the end of his dealings with us. At the turn of the year, we start out on a fresh stage of our journey.

1. "Not as yet come"—but certainly farther on than we were.
2. "Not as yet come"—but assuredly on the way.
3. "Not as yet come"—but even now we may know the joys of journey's end.

Adapted.
—J. Ellis

111. WAYSIDE ALTARS

"Take heed to thyself that thou offer not thy burnt offerings in every place that thou seest."
DEUT. 12:13-14

1. There is the wayside altar of pleasure.
    Let us take heed that we do not make our offering there.
2. There is the wayside altar of business.
    Let us take heed that we do not present our offering there.
3. There is the wayside altar of fame.
    Let us take heed that we do not offer our sacrifice there.
4. There is only one altar at which we must make our offering, and that is not a wayside altar, but the altar of him who is the way.

—Arthur Stanley Wheelock

112. THE TWO PRODIGALS

"This our son." DEUT. 21:20
"This my son." LUKE 15:24

There are two prodigals in the Bible—one in the Old Testament and the other in the New. On the whole, their characters are pretty much alike, yet the treatment accorded to them is revealingly different.

It presents a threefold contrast:

1. The contrast between law and love
2. The contrast between publicity and privacy
3. The contrast between punishment and pardon

113. THE MINISTRY OF PROTECTION

"When thou buildest a new house, then thou shalt make a battlement for thy roof, that thou bring not blood upon thine house, if any man fall from thence."   Deut. 22:8

Here we have an early experiment in social security, a safety measure, designed to prevent accidents.

Notice that in our text:

1. The protective parapet is around the roof, where in the East men recline and enjoy their leisure. This teaches us that there is no area of life, even the pleasant and peaceful, without its dangers.
2. It is worth comment that the battlement on the roof did not curtail movement, but made it possible. The vision and delight enjoyed by those on the rooftop were possible because the boundary which shut them in, shut danger out.
3. The parapet required by divine law as a safety measure naturally increased the cost of the house. Life is ever more valuable than property. There has never been any personal or social improvement without cost.

—Wilfred Shepherd, *Noughts and Crosses*

114. LEARNING

"Learn to fear the Lord your God."

Deut. 31:13

1. We learn by the example of others.
    Some men, it has been said, are not guiding lights but warning beacons.
2. We learn by our own mistakes.
3. We learn under the guidance of the Holy Spirit.

115. THE BEWILDERED EAGLET

"As an eagle stirreth up her nest, fluttereth over her young, spreadeth abroad her wings, taketh them, beareth them on her wings."

DEUT. 32:11

The eagle is not only remarkable for its easy flight, but for the care of its young. It takes trouble to cover its nest of twigs and boughs with downy lining, so as to make it soft for the young eaglet that is to be fledged and nourished there. But after a while it behaves in a strange and, to the eaglet, inexplicable way. It tears the down out of its nest and allows the thorns to pierce the young bird until it is forced to fling itself out of the nest altogether.

1. God, like the eagle, stirs our nest.
2. The stirring of the nest is sure to appear strange to us.
3. Our Lord mars the nest because of the purpose which led him to make it.

—W. Y. Fullerton, *God's Highway*

116. THE WRECKING OF THE NEST

"As an eagle stirreth up her nest, fluttereth over her young, spreadeth abroad her wings, taketh them, beareth them on her wings."

DEUT. 32:11

Note here:

1. The discipline of disturbance.
   Think of God wrecking the comfortable securities of:
      a) the soul.
      b) the family.
      c) the nation.
      d) the Church.
      e) the world.
2. The fall which is preparatory to the flight.
      a) the fall of repentance and the flight of faith
      b) the fall of humility and the flight of holiness

> c) the fall of worship and the flight of praise

3. The invisible supports vouchsafed to living faith.

117. DEEP DOWN

"The deep that coucheth beneath."

DEUT. 33:13

Consider the deep that coucheth:

1. In ourselves
2. In our fellows
3. In life itself
4. In worship
5. In the scriptures
6. In the cross of Christ

—Harold T. Barrow

118. THE ETERNAL REFUGE

"The eternal God is thy refuge, and underneath are the everlasting arms." DEUT. 33:27

1. The eternal God is the refuge from the insoluble mysteries of life.
2. The eternal God is the refuge from all the illusions of life.
3. The eternal God is the refuge from all human limitations and the sense of insignificance.
4. The eternal God is the refuge from the sense of sin and loneliness.
5. The eternal God is the refuge in the last great adventure into the future life.

—Thomas W. Davidson,
The Fascination of the Unknown

119. THE ARMS OF THE AGES

"Underneath are the everlasting arms."

DEUT. 33:27

We often speak of "the long arm of the law," but the arms of grace are far longer.

57

1. The arms underneath me are the arms underneath everything.
2. Once nestling in those arms we are safe for ever. They are "everlasting arms."
3. If the arms of God are around me, then he himself is near me and his face is toward me.
4. It is possible to realize the enfolding rest of the unfailing arms under the most adverse circumstances.

—W. Y. Fullerton, *God's Highway*

120. WHEN YOU FEEL LIKE GOING UNDER

"Underneath are the everlasting arms."
DEUT. 33:27

"His understanding is infinite." Ps. 147:5

"Undertake for me." ISA. 38:14

Recollect that:

1. He is underneath.
2. He is understanding.
3. He is undertaking.

—Robert Barr, *In Sweet Remembrance*

121. WHY BE A CHRISTIAN?

"Who is like unto thee, O people saved by the Lord?" DEUT. 33:29

Is there not something like the sound of a trumpet in that? Here surely is a word of God to stir and thrill our hearts.

For you see what it does. It takes religion, the life that is lived for God, and it lifts it up before the eyes of the world, and cries: "There—can you beat that?"

I am prepared to maintain that:

1. The Christian life is happier than any other.
2. The Christian life is harder than any other.
3. The Christian life is holier than any other.
4. The Christian life is more hopeful than any other.

—James S. Stewart, *The Gates of New Life*

122. THE SECRET OF HAPPINESS

"Happy art thou, O Israel."   DEUT. 33:29

What is the secret of happiness? It consists mainly of four things:

1. A clear conscience, an absolutely straight and clean life
2. The faculty of living a day at a time
3. Making some real contribution to life
4. Regular use of the means of grace

—G. T. Bellhouse

JOSHUA

123. A NEW YEAR MEDITATION

"As I was with Moses, so I will be with thee."

JOSH. 1:5

1. The eternal God is the link between the dead and the living.
   "With Moses . . . with thee."
2. The living God is the link between the past and the future.
   "As I was . . . so I will be."
3. The unchangeable God is the link between the known and the unknown.
   "As I was . . . so I will be."
4. The all-sufficient God is the link between the great and the small.
   "With Moses . . . with thee."

—Scottish Free Church Record

124. COURAGE FOR TODAY

"Be strong and of a good courage."

JOSH. 1:6

This was God's challenge to Joshua and it is his challenge to us.

Notice:

1. Courage is the child of conviction.
2. Courage is the brother of faith.
3. Courage is the father of enterprise.
4. Courage is the grandfather of achievement.

Adapted.
—J. R. Hill

125. THE RED CORD

"Behold, when we come into the land, thou shalt bind this line of scarlet thread in the window."
JOSH. 2:18

Note:

1. A red cord hangs in the window of nature.
2. A red cord hangs in the window of the Christian faith.
3. A red cord hangs in the window of personal spiritual experience.
4. A red cord hangs in the window of heaven itself.

126. THE FASCINATION OF THE UNKNOWN

"Ye have not passed this way heretofore."
JOSH. 3:4

1. The fascination of the unknown makes a fitting appeal to our love of adventure in common life.
2. The fascination of the unknown needs to be met and mastered by the presence of a living faith in God.
3. The fascination of the unknown gives a widespread interest in life and supplies ample opportunity to find the way of helpful service.

—Thomas W. Davidson,
The Fascination of the Unknown

127. CROSSING THE RIVER

JOSH. 3:15-17

1. Obstacles, when touched, vanish.
"As they that bare the ark were come unto Jordan, and the feet of the priests that

bare the ark were dipped in the brim of the water, . . . that the waters which came down from above stood and rose up upon an heap." (vss. 15-16)

2. Everything that God does is well finished. "All the Israelites passed over on dry ground." (vs. 17)

3. Between us and success and prosperity there is always a river to be crossed.
"Jordan overfloweth all his banks all the time of harvest." (vs. 15b)

—T. De Witt Talmage

128. THE LITTLE THINGS FOR WHICH MEN SELL THEIR SOULS

A noted evangelist once declared that nothing would astound us so much on the day of doom as the paltry things for which men had sold their souls.

Consider three biblical illustrations of this.

1. Achan
"When I saw among the spoils a goodly Babylonish garment, and two hundred shekels of silver." Josh. 7:21.
This may have seemed quite a lot to the poor man at the time, but how little it was in comparison with the worth of his life!

2. Gehazi
"Give them, I pray thee, a talent of silver, and two changes of garments."
II Kings 5:22

3. Judas
"They covenanted with him for thirty pieces of silver." Matt. 26:15
"Tramp, tramp, tramp! How the centuries march along," cried D. L. Moody. "But do you think Judas ever forgets those thirty pieces?"

Still as of old
Man by himself is priced;

61

For thirty pieces Judas sold
His soul, not Christ.

129. THINGS UNDONE

(A Year-End Sermon Outline)

"He left nothing undone of all that the Lord commanded Moses." Josh. 11:15

"This year omissions have distressed me more than anything." So speaks Andrew A. Bonar, concluding one of the years of his life. How many of us at this moment are similarly distressed!

1. The things undone are many.
2. The things undone are often the things of greatest consequence.
3. The things undone are things for which we must be held responsible.

—W. L. Watkinson, *The Blind Spot*

130. THE MAN WITH A MOUNTAIN ON HIS MIND

"Now therefore give me this mountain."

Josh. 14:12

This is Caleb's request to Joshua. Caleb is eighty-five, but he still possesses the spirit of the pioneer. Notice:

1. His dauntlessness

   The mountain represented difficulty and danger.

2. His singleheartedness

   It was the mountain he wanted, and nothing but the mountain would suffice.

3. His disinterestedness

   The mountain was not as desirable, in other people's opinion, as other places Caleb might have had, nevertheless he sued for it.

4. His farsightedness

   The mountain possessed strategic importance. Once gained, it could be a springboard for further conquest.

131. SPRINGS OF WATER

"*Thou hast given me a south land; give me also springs of water.*" JOSH. 15:19

 1. Springs of water mean abundance.
 2. Springs of water mean beauty.
 3. Springs of water mean music.

—D. M. JOSS

132. PROGRESS BY DIVINE PROVIDENCE

"*Forasmuch as the Lord hath blessed me hitherto.*" JOSH. 17:14

We must:

 1. Review the Lord's plans.
  a) Realize that leadership is with the Lord.
  b) Recognize the appointments of his plans.
  c) Rehearse the special events of God's intervention.
 2. Reason to the Lord's purposes.
  a) His past gives pledge of his purpose.
  b) His continuance is the ground of our confidence.
  c) His resources are the assurance of our successes.
 3. Respond to the Lord's appeals.
  a) The past is but a suggestion of God's further plans.
  b) In enlarged enterprises he privileges us with a part.
  c) His projects can only be discovered by prayer.

—W. B. Riley, *The Preacher and His Preaching*

JUDGES

133. WHERE GREAT RESOLVES ARE MADE

"By the watercourses of Reuben there were great resolves." JUDG. 5:16

1. New Year is a watercourse at which great resolves are made.
2. Conversion is a watercourse at which great resolves are made.
3. The Church is a watercourse at which great resolves are made.

134. THE BATTLE WITHOUT A SWORD

"And the three companies blew the trumpets, and brake the pitchers, and held the lamps in their left hands." JUDG. 7:20

Alexander Maclaren characterized this as "the battle without a sword." What curious weapons of war its soldiers carried—trumpets, pitchers, lamps!

These hint at the qualities we still require in the good fight of faith.

1. Boldness
   The trumpet speaks of that.
2. Brokenness
   The shattered pitcher speaks of that.
3. Brightness
   The lamp speaks of that.

135. WHAT SHALL WE DO TO THE CHILD?
A CHRISTMAS SERMON OUTLINE

"What we shall do unto the child that shall be born?" JUDG. 13:8

1. The answer of hostility
   Herod's reply: "Let him be destroyed."
2. The answer of indifference
   The Bethlehem inn-keeper's reply: "Let him be ignored."

3. The answer of commitment
Simeon's reply: "Let him be accepted."
—James S. Stewart

136. ALL THESE THINGS

"If the Lord were pleased to kill us, he would not have received a burnt offering . . . neither would he have shewed us all these things." Judg. 13:23
Here is a sheet anchor when we find ourselves tossing pitifully on some wild sea of God-denying troubles.

What are some of the things God has shown us?
1. His interesting world
2. His inspired Word
3. His incarnate Son
—Robert Barr, *In Sweet Remembrance*

137. UNCONSCIOUS CHANGES IN HUMAN LIFE

Many of the vital processes in our bodies operate without our being aware of it. Breathing is largely unconscious. That is well; for, if we had to think before drawing every breath, we should not be able to think of anything else. The action of a healthy heart is unconscious. The normal digestive functions are unconscious.

So in our souls. There may be:
1. Unconscious deterioration.
"Samson . . . wist not that the Lord was departed from him." Judg. 16:20
2. Unconscious sanctification.
"Moses wist not that the skin of his face shone." Exod. 34:29
3. Unconscious emancipation.
"[Peter] wist not that it was true which was done by the angel." Acts 12:9

138. THE ECLIPSE OF HUMAN POWER

"And he [Samson] awoke out of his sleep, and said, I will go out as at other times before, and

65

shake myself. And he wist not that the Lord was departed from him." JUDG. 16:20

This eclipse of power was gradual—first partial, then total. We can trace the deterioration in Samson's character thus:

1. We can see great powers devoted to frivolous and petty uses.
2. We can see a man devoting his powers to his own amusement.
3. We can see a man forgetful of the true source of his strength.

—W. J. Rowlands, *The Suburban Christ*

139. HOW SIN WORKS OUT

"But the Philistines took him, and put out his eyes, and brought him down to Gaza, and bound him with fetters of brass; and he did grind in the prison house." JUDG. 16:21

1. The binding
2. The blinding
3. The grinding

—T. Harwood Pattison,
The Making of the Sermon

RUTH

140. THE LORD GIVING BREAD

"The Lord had visited his people in giving them bread." RUTH 1:6

1. He does this in his material provision.
2. He does this in the Bible.
3. He does this in the Sacrament.

141. HOW THE YEARS TELL

"Is this Naomi?" RUTH 1:19

1. A change in her aspect led to this exclamation.

2. A change in her fortune helped to draw from the crowd this word of surprise.
3. A change in her spirit brought her within range of such a cry as this.

—David Burns, *The Song of the Well*

142. THE GOOD FORTUNE OF RUTH
RUTH 2

Here we see her:

1. Seeking supplies from the harvest of Boaz.
2. Finding favor in the heart of Boaz.
3. Receiving refreshment from the hand of Boaz.
4. Saved and satisfied by the hospitality of Boaz.

—D. Hogg

143. THE WINGS OF GOD
"The Lord God of Israel, under whose wings thou art come to trust." RUTH 2:12

1. They are swift wings.
2. They are broad wings.
3. They are strong wings.
4. They are gentle wings.

—T. De Witt Talmage

144. THE WELCOME GUEST
"And Boaz said unto her [Ruth], At mealtime come thou hither, and eat of the bread, and dip thy morsel in the vinegar." RUTH 2:14

1. A foreigner and yet welcome at the table
2. A gleaner and yet welcome at the table
3. A kinswoman and therefore welcome at the table
4. Beloved and so doubly welcome at the table

145. THE DAILY TAKINGS
"Where hast thou gleaned today?" RUTH 2:19

1. What have you gleaned intellectually?
   What nourishing book have you read?
2. What have you gleaned experientially?
   What have you learned from life?

3. What have you gleaned spiritually?
   What enrichment has come to you from
   Bible study, prayer, fellowship?
4. What have you gleaned evangelistically?
   What soul have you won for Christ?

146. CHRIST'S RIGHT TO REDEEM US

"This man is one that hath the right to redeem."
RUTH 2:20 E. R. V. Margin

1. Christ has the right to redeem us because
   it was he who made us.
2. Christ has the right to redeem us because
   he became one of us.
3. Christ has the right to redeem us because
   he died to do so.

I SAMUEL

147. MISUNDERSTOOD

I SAM. 1:12-14

Hannah was misunderstood:

1. In the place where she might most have
   looked for understanding.
   "The temple."
2. By the person from whom she might most
   have looked for understanding.
   "The high priest."
3. In the act and attitude in which she might
   most have looked for understanding.
   Prayer.

148. SAMUEL AND HIS LORD

1. Lent unto the Lord
   "Therefore also I have lent him to the
   Lord." I Sam. 1:28

2. Listening to the Lord
   "Speak; for thy servant heareth."
   I Sam. 3:10

3. Laboring for the Lord
   "And the child Samuel ministered unto
   the Lord." I Sam. 3:1
   —David Hogg

149. THE GOD WHO KILLS

"*The Lord killeth.*" I SAM. 2:6

That is not the way in which we normally think
of God, nor is it the sort of activity which we
commonly ascribe to him. Yet here in this ancient
song he is spoken of in this unconventional
manner. "The Lord killeth."

Is there truth in the statement, apart from the
obvious fact that in God's hands are the issues
of all life?

Yes!

1. There is the killing of redemption.
2. There is the killing of repentance.
3. There is the killing of resignation.

150. IN TOUCH WITH REALITY

"When the Philistines took the ark of God, they
brought it into the house of Dagon, and set it by
Dagon. And when they of Ashdod arose early on
the morrow, behold, Dagon was fallen upon his
face to the ground before the ark of the Lord. And
they took Dagon, and set him in his place again.
And when they arose early on the morrow morning, behold, Dagon was fallen upon his face to
the ground before the ark of the Lord; and the
head of Dagon and both the palms of his hands
were cut off upon the threshold; only the stump
of Dagon was left to him." I SAM. 5:2-4

Dagon was a man-made god. He was unreal.
The ark was a man-made symbol, but it was
God-given. It was in touch with reality. Here we
see a duel between the true God and the false.

69

Let me point out two or three principles which are written deep into this truth-revealing story.

1. God's truth cannot be compromised.
2. God's will cannot be subordinated.
3. The presence of God cannot be avoided.

—Hugh T. Kerr, *The Highway of Life*

151. THE LANDMARKS OF LIFE

"Then Samuel took a stone, and set it between Mizpah and Shen, and called the name of it Ebenezer, saying, Hitherto hath the Lord helped us." I SAM. 7:12

Every life has its landmarks. Such memorials may commemorate the triumphs or the tragedies, the successes or the failures, of personal experience. But the finest landmarks are those which call attention to what God has been to us and has done for us. Such a stone of memory was that set up by Samuel.

1. A landmark is a good place from which to look back.
   "Hitherto"
2. A landmark is a good place from which to look up.
   "The Lord"
3. A landmark is a good place from which to look forward.
   It says to us, "As God has helped, so he will help."

—Thomas W. Davidson,
The Fascination of the Unknown

152. THE GREAT THINGS GOD HAS DONE FOR US

"Only fear the Lord, and serve him in truth with all your heart: for consider how great things he hath done for you." I SAM. 12:24

Consider that:

1. God has done great things for us physically.
2. God has done great things for us mentally.

3. God has done great things for us morally and spiritually.
4. God has done great things for us socially.

153. GOD'S VIEW OF US, AND MAN'S

"The Lord seeth not as man seeth; for man looketh on the outward appearance, but the Lord looketh on the heart." I Sam. 16:7

Here we have suggested a threefold contrast:

1. Man sees the physical, God sees the spiritual.
2. Man sees the present, God sees the future.
3. Man sees what we have done, God sees what we meant to do.

154. THE MAN GOD CHOOSES

"The Lord said, Arise, anoint him: for this is he."
I Sam. 16:12

It is always thrilling to be picked out from among others for some special privilege or distinction. The schoolboy knows that when his master selects him for some coveted honor; the soldier knows it when his commanding officer chooses him for some post of peculiar peril; the bride knows it when her betrothed binds her to himself in preference to all other possible partners.

But what if there should be such a thing as being chosen of God? There is! The principle of election is for ever at work. You find it in nature, in the Bible, in history.

The man whom God chooses—what sort of person is he, on the evidence of this ancient story?

1. He does not judge himself worthy of the high honor.

   If David had thought himself eligible for kingship, he wouldn't have been content to tend the sheep.

2. He is not often deemed by others deserving of the distinction.

   Jesse esteemed his youngest son so lightly that he did not even arrange for him to

have a place in the queue when the
crown was to be bestowed.

3. He is one who, as time goes on, invariably
justifies the divine choice in his life.

Eliab, Abinadab, Shammah—David's big
brothers—how they outshone him that
day in stature and maturity, but today the
Biblical Encyclopaedia dismisses their
whole lives in a sentence or two, while the
career of David is recorded on page after
page. Yes! God's choice was justified in
the end.

155. DAVID'S THREE ANOINTINGS — AND CHRIST'S

*"Then Samuel took the horn of oil, and anointed
him in the midst of his brethren."*

I SAM. 16:13

*"And the men of Judah came, and there they
anointed David king over the house of Judah."*

II SAM. 2:4

*"So all the elders of Israel came to the king to
Hebron . . . and they anointed David king over
Israel."* II SAM. 5:3

1. David was thrice anointed king.
   a) In the midst of his family
   b) In the midst of his tribe
   c) In the midst of the nation
2. In this he is like Christ, who is also to have
   a threefold anointing.
   a) Christ must be anointed king per-
      sonally—in the individual heart.
   b) Christ must be anointed king ec-
      clesiastically—in his Church.
   c) Christ must be anointed king uni-
      versally—in the world at large.

156. AN IDEAL FRIENDSHIP

*"The soul of Jonathan was knit with the soul of
David, and Jonathan loved him as his own soul."*

I SAM. 18:1

These two names, David and Jonathan, have been

a proverb in every age for true and brave friendship. Damon and Pythias, in the world of classic story, are not worthy to be put beside them, while the love of a Hallam and a Tennyson, enshrined in the poem "In Memoriam," belongs at least as much to the sphere of elegiac literature as to that of real life.

What were the marks of this ideal friendship?

1. Its disinterested quality
2. Its glowing hero worship
3. Its expression in service
4. Its renunciation

—Hugh Ross Mackintosh, *Sermons*

157. A CLASSIC FRIENDSHIP

There have been several wonderful friendships in the history of the world. But none greater than that of David and Jonathan. Note three things about it.

1. It was a covenanted friendship.
   "Then Jonathan and David made a covenant, because he loved him as his own soul." I Sam. 18:3
2. It was a courageous friendship.
   Look at the picture of Jonathan in the palace at the feast of the new moon. "Then Jonathan said to David, To morrow is the new moon: and thou shalt be missed, because thy seat will be empty."
   I Sam. 20:18
3. It was a ceaseless friendship.
   "The Lord be between me and thee, and between my seed and thy seed for ever."
   I Sam. 20:42
   —George Allen

158. THE MYSTIC STEP

"There is but a step between me and death."
I Sam. 20:3

Note:

1. It is a certain step.

2. It is an uncertain step.
3. It is a final step.
4. It is a parting step.
5. It is a solitary step.
6. It is a solemn step.

—T. Dunlop

159. BLESSED ADVICE

"And David said to Abigail, Blessed be the Lord God of Israel, which sent thee this day to meet me: And blessed be thy advice."

I SAM. 25:32-33

How did she manage to cool David down?
What was the line she took?

1. She appealed to his reason.
"Ah, my lord, pay no attention to that worthless creature, Nabal!—he is like his name. 'Nabal,' 'Churl,' is his name, and churl is his nature!" I Sam. 25:25!

Moffatt

2. She appealed to the future.
3. She appealed to David's religion.

—G. T. Bellhouse

160. PLAYING THE FOOL

"Behold, I have played the fool, and have erred exceedingly." I SAM. 26:21

In the Bible are to be found many kinds of fools. Four classes we shall specially consider.

1. The atheistic fool
"The fool hath said in his heart, There is no God." Ps. 14:1
2. The conceited fool
"I have played the fool." I Sam. 26:21
3. The selfish fool
"Thou fool." Luke 12:20
4. The careless fool
Exemplified by the foolish bridesmaids.

Matt. 25:1-13

—Russell M. Brougher

II SAMUEL

161. WHY ABNER DIED AS A FOOL

"Died Abner as a fool dieth?" II Sam. 3:33

1. Because of his unwise policy.
   He tried to keep in with Saul and David.
2. Because of his unused powers.
   He didn't try to defend himself.
3. Because of his unappropriated privileges.
   There were cities of refuge in which he might have been safe, but he was killed in the shadow of the city gate.

—Peter Connolly

162. AS ONE OF THE KING'S SONS

"Eat at my table, as one of the king's sons."
II Sam. 9:11
"Eat and drink at my table . . . and sit on thrones."
Luke 22:30

The tables mentioned in our texts have many things in common. Consider three such things:

1. They both speak of a seeking king.
2. They both speak of a shrinking soul.
3. They both speak of an accepted sonship.

—Robert Barr, *In Sweet Remembrance*

163. THE FIVE POINTS OF CALVINISM

"So Mephibosheth dwelt in Jerusalem: for he did eat continually at the king's table; and was lame on both his feet." II Sam. 9:13

James Denney roundly declared that there are no doctrines in the Old Testament. Evidently, an old Puritan preacher disagreed with him, for in this verse he ingeniously finds the five points of Calvinism.

1. The doctrine of human depravity.
   "Mephibosheth . . . was lame."
2. The doctrine of total depravity.
   He was "lame on both his feet."

75

3. The doctrine of justification.
   He "dwelt in Jerusalem."
4. The doctrine of adoption.
   "He did eat continually at the king's table."
5. The doctrine of the perseverance of the saints.
   "He did eat continually at the king's table."

164. DAVID'S DARK DOUBLE CRIME

"And David said unto Nathan, I have sinned against the Lord. And Nathan said unto David, The Lord also hath put away thy sin; thou shalt not die." II Sam. 12:13

The Bible does not hide the blots on the lives of its best and bravest characters. It paints them, as Cromwell bade the artist paint him, "warts and all."

What are the lessons we may draw from this story of David's dreadful lapse?

1. David's sin occurred when he was a king and not when he was a shepherd boy. A life of luxury and ease exposes us especially to temptation.
2. David's sin involved others.
3. David's sin, although sincerely repented of, had inevitable consequences.
4. David's sin was nevertheless forgiven.

165. THE BEYOND

"I shall go to him, but he shall not return to me."
II Sam. 12:23

We have here:

1. The unreturning dead.
   "He shall not return to me."
2. The uncontinuing living.
   "I shall go to him."
3. The unseverable reunion.
   "*I* shall go to *him*."

166. WHY A KING'S SON SHOULD LOOK WELL

"*Why art thou, being the king's son, lean from day to day?*" II Sam. 13:4

1. A king's son should look well because of his father.
2. A king's son should look well because of his fare.
3. A king's son should look well because of his finery.

167. THE PRODIGAL PARENT

"*Deal gently for my sake with the young man.*" II Sam. 18:5

Though Absalom has been called "the prodigal son of the Old Testament" the resemblance is purely superficial, for this particular prodigal son had a prodigal father.

In this incident we see:

1. Misplaced devotion.
2. Delegated responsibility.
3. Squandered influence.

—Tom Dick, *Expository Times*

168. THE FERRYBOAT

"*And there went over a ferryboat to carry over the king's household, and to do what he thought good.*" II Sam. 19:18

1. There is a river of decision.
   We need a ferryboat there.
   It is the grace of God.
2. There is a river of difficulty.
   We need a ferryboat there.
   It is the power of God.
3. There is a river of death.
   We shall need a ferryboat there.
   It is the life of God.

169. MEN OF IRON

"*The man that shall touch them must be fenced with iron.*" II Sam. 23:7

Was it, do you think, mere coincidence that at one time two of the leading men in the world had names linked with this strong metal—Eisenhower, Stalin?

Note:

1. God wants men as strong as iron.
2. God seeks such men though, like iron, they may have to be dug from the depths.
3. God can make the most effective use of these men when, white-hot with love for him, they are malleable and manipulable in his hand.

170. DAVID'S OFFERING

"*Three mighty men . . . drew water out of the well of Bethlehem . . . and brought it to David: nevertheless he would not drink thereof, but poured it out unto the Lord.*" II SAM. 23:16

It was:

1. A common thing—water.
2. A costly thing—secured at jeopardy of lives.
3. A consecrated thing—poured out unto the Lord.

—James Smith, *Handfuls on Purpose*

I KINGS

171. THE ART OF SPOILING CHILDREN

"*His father had not displeased him at any time in saying, Why hast thou done so?*" I KINGS 1:6

We are not surprised to learn that this lad went wrong. His father did not trouble to correct him. The boy was permitted to do just as he liked, and it is little wonder that he ended up as he did. Why did the father adopt this ruinous attitude? What was the reason?

1. Was it indifference?
2. Was it indulgence?
3. Was it incompetence?

Whatever it was, it was fatal!

172. GOD'S BOUNTY FOR ANOTHER YEAR

"The Lord appeared to Solomon . . . and God said, Ask what I shall give thee." I Kings 3:5

That is the staggering offer with which God meets us on the threshold of the year. Of all possible gifts, what shall we welcome most from God?

1. We had better ask for courage.
2. We shall need patience.
3. Surely we shall want to ask for faith.

—James Munn, *Expository Times*

173. THE UNASKED BLESSINGS

"I have also given thee that which thou hast not asked." I Kings 3:13

Have you ever considered the unasked blessings of life? Quite often we hear folk talking about the prayers that have been answered, and these are very striking. But we rarely hear about answers being given to prayers which have never been prayed; yet, when we come to think about it, these are the most profound of all.

1. Consider the unasked blessings of nature.
2. Consider the unasked blessings of providence.
3. Consider the unasked blessings of grace.

—C. Leslie Brewer

174. GOD'S TEMPLES OF SILENCE

"There was neither hammer nor ax nor any tool of iron heard in the house, while it was in building." I Kings 6:7

We may learn from this incident:

1. Many of God's best gifts come to us silently.

2. God's ways are often misunderstood and mis-
interpreted.
3. God makes use of silence in constructing
the temple of the soul.

—D. C. Mitchell, *The Nonsense of Neutrality*

175. UNREALIZED PURPOSES

"*And the Lord said unto David my father,
Whereas it was in thine heart to build an house
unto my name, thou didst well that it was in thine
heart. Nevertheless thou shalt not build the
house; but thy son that shall come forth out of
thy loins, he shall build the house unto my
name.*" I KINGS 8:17-19

Here is an incident which supplies abundant material for reflection.

Note:

1. The purpose which was denied.
2. That every man has his limitations even in
God's service.
3. David's behavior under this disappointment:
   a) no complaint.
   b) co-operation.
4. That it is good to have high desires and
aims though they should never be realized.

—Charles Brown, *God and Man*

176. HOME

"*Come home with me, and refresh thyself.*"
I KINGS 13:7

Home is a grand old Anglo-Saxon word, and no
other in our language is so expressive and suggestive.

1. Home ought to be haven amid the storms
of life.
2. Home ought to be an oasis amid the weari-
ness of life. It must never be a mere mirage.
3. Home ought to be an enquiry office amid
the problems of life.

—W. C. Wright

177. WHAT LIFE OUGHT TO BE

"As the Lord God of Israel liveth, before whom I stand." I KINGS 17:1

1. Life may be a constant vision of God's presence.
   "As the Lord liveth before whom I stand."
2. Life should echo with the voice of the divine command.
   "Before whom I stand"—as a servant awaiting his commands.
3. Life, for us, must be full of conscious obedience.

—Alexander Maclaren

178. BETWEEN TWO OPINIONS

"How long halt ye between two opinions?"
I KINGS 18:21

Do you recall this robust saying of an old preacher? "The man who does not form an opinion is a sluggard; the man who cannot form an opinion is a fool; the man who will not form an opinion is a coward."

Note:

1. Some have no opinions.
   For example, French courtiers addressing their king: "Sire, what are our opinions?"
2. Some are of two opinions.
3. Some have the wrong opinion.
4. Some, thank God, have the right opinion.

179. AT THE CROSSROADS

"How long halt ye between two opinions?"
I KINGS 18:21

1. The divine alternative
   "If the Lord be God, follow him: but if Baal, then follow him." (vs. 21b)
2. The divine prerogative
   "The God that answereth by fire, let him be God." (vs. 24)

3. The divine imperative
   "If the Lord be God, follow him."
   (vs. 21b)
   —Stephen Olford, *Christianity and You*

180. INDECISION

"And Elijah came unto all the people, and said, How long halt ye between two opinions?"
I KINGS 18:21

1. There are two entirely distinct schemes of life.
2. These schemes of life are utterly irreconcilable.
3. It is intolerable to waver between the two.
   a) Think of the misery of indecision.
   b) Think of the perils of indecision.

—W. L. Watkinson,
The Education of the Heart

181. THE PRETEXTS OF INDECISION

"How long halt ye between two opinions? if the Lord be God, follow him; but if Baal, then follow him. And the people answered him not a word."
I KINGS 18:21

What are these undecided ones waiting for?

1. Some wait for clearer light.
2. Some wait for a more powerful impulse.
3. Some wait for a convenient season.

—W. L. Watkinson,
The Education of the Heart

182. THE GOD WHO ANSWERS BY FIRE

"The God that answereth by fire, let him be God."
I KINGS 18:24

Three facts about fire may be noted here:

1. Fire flashes forth from friction.
   So it often is with the prophet when "the steel of his passion strikes the flint of life."
2. Fire communicates itself by contact.

3. Fire transforms to its own nature whatever it touches.

183. THERE IS NOTHING

"And [he] said to his servants, Go up now, look toward the sea. And he went up, and looked, and said, There is nothing. And he said, Go again seven times." I KINGS 18:43

"And [he] said, There is nothing. And he said, Go again." That furnishes the point of real interest in this famous story. I draw three deductions therefrom:

1. In the face of explicit promises, the Lord for a time may allow us to see no signs.
2. God's promises are better than signs in the sky.
3. Failure is an unknown experience for faith.
   —Merton S. Rice, *The American Pulpit*

184. THE "UNANSWERED" PRAYERS OF THE BIBLE

"*It is enough; now, O Lord, take away my life; for I am not better than my fathers.*"
I KINGS 19:4
"*O My Father, if it be possible, let this cup pass from me.*" MATT. 26:39
"*For this thing I besought the Lord thrice, that it might depart from me.*" II COR. 12:8

One of the greatest problems of the spiritual life is the problem of what we call "unanswered" prayer. Properly speaking, of course, there is no such thing as unanswered prayer. God always answers in one way or another. His answer may be "Yes" or it may be "No" or it may be "Not yet," but in each case it is an answer all the same. Consider three "unanswered" prayers in the Bible and the reasons for the replies given.

1. Elijah's prayer was "unanswered" because God wanted to do something better for him. He begged for a grave in the wilderness; God

83

planned to carry him by a whirlwind to the skies.
2. Christ's prayer in Gethsemane was "unanswered" because God wanted to do something better *through* him.
3. Paul's prayer was "unanswered" because God wanted to do something better *in* him.

185. RETREAT

"What doest thou here, Elijah?" I Kings 19:9

No man in the Bible looks less like a coward than Elijah. Yet here in this narrative we see him showing as clean a pair of heels as ever cobbler fitted to human footwear. His panic-stricken flight terminated in a lonely cave amid the wilds of Horeb. And there God put to him the stabbing and startling question: "What doest thou here?"

That question may suggest three others which we may profitably put to ourselves.

1. Where am I?
2. Why am I here?
3. What am I doing here?

—Arthur Mursell

186. THE MYSTIC VOICE

"A still small voice." I Kings 19:12

Conscience has been defined as "the still small voice that makes us feel still smaller." It is likewise the voice which, if we obey it, makes us great.

"If we obey it." Everything depends on that. Are we willing to follow its guidance? Note:

1. Guidance is not the mere light of reason.
2. Guidance is more than the direction of expedients.
3. Guidance is more than personal judgment confirmed by that of others.
4. Guidance is not just the pointing pressure of circumstances.

5. Guidance is nothing less than God's voice within.

187. THE OMNIPRESENT ONE

"The Lord is God of the hills, but he is not God of the valleys." I KINGS 20:28

So the Syrians said. To their mind the god of a people belonged solely to them, and he had power only in a certain place. Last spring, on the heights of Samaria, a handful of Israel's youths had struck their hosts with panic; and the reason must have been that their God had his seat on the hills. Next time they would take care that the battle would be in a valley.

We, of course, know God to be everywhere alike. Nevertheless, we are not at one in our attitude to the assertion of the text.

1. Some of us revive the saying.
2. Some of us reverse the saying.
3. Some of us revise the saying.

—David Burns, *The Song of the Well*

188. THE CASE OF THE ESCAPED PRISONER

"As thy servant was busy here and there, he was gone." I KINGS 20:40

1. Each of us has received some specific charge from God.
2. To discharge that particular duty is the true work of our life.
3. However active we may be in other directions, if we fail at this point, we fail altogether.

189. THE REALMS OF CHANCE

"A certain man drew a bow at a venture."
I KINGS 22:34

How heavy do you think were the odds against that arrow finding Ahab's body? I want you to watch that arrow very closely. It suggests the element of chance that so often seems to be in the life of the world.

Consider:

1. The things we suffer.

To other eyes they look like evil chances, but God desires them to have for ourselves a deeper meaning.

2. The things we do.

We do deeds that may be the little causes of great events.

3. The things we cannot understand.

Earthquakes, storms, pestilences, famines, and disasters look more like the reign of fate or chance than the will of a loving Father. Yet the duty of the believing heart is to live near to God, and to look at all that seems most like chance and accident in the light of his wisdom and love.

—J. M. E. Ross, *The Christian Standpoint*

II KINGS

190. OUR ATTITUDE TO TRADITION

"He took up also the mantel of Elijah that fell from him." II Kings 2:13

1. The mantle of Elijah is a trust to be handled with reverence and responsibility.
2. The mantle of Elijah is a challenge: it is there not to be looked at and admired but adapted and worn.
3. The mantle of Elijah is the symbol of a spirit, a spirit that must be kept alive.

—R. Leonard Small, *Expository Times*

191. DIG TRENCHES

"Make this valley full of ditches. For thus saith the Lord, ye shall not see wind, neither shall ye

see rain; yet that valley shall be filled with water,
that ye may drink, both ye, and your cattle, and
your beasts." II KINGS 3:16-17

1. Dig the trench of a creed for the water of
   living personal faith.
2. Dig the trench of a disciplined prayer life
   for the water of spiritual power.
3. Dig the trench of dedicated service for the
   experience of divine reinforcement.
4. Dig the trench of ecclesiastical organization
   for the water of religious revival.

192. FEMININE GREATNESS

"And it fell on a day, that Elisha passed to
Shunem, where was a great woman."

II KINGS 4:8

From this narrative we learn that:

1. Greatness is not limited to great cities or
   great houses.
2. Greatness does not exempt from great
   trouble.
3. Greatness always carries its sorrows to a
   greater.
4. It is not only for the great that God does
   great things.

—Unknown

193. CURING THE CAPTAIN

"Now Naaman, captain of the host of the king of
Syria, was a great man with his master . . . a
mighty man of valour, but he was a leper."

II KINGS 5:1-14

1. The expected appearance
   "Behold, I thought, He will surely come
   out to me." (vs. 11)
2. The disappointing substitute
   "Elisha sent a messenger unto him."
   (vs. 10)
3. The unpopular communication
   "Go and wash in Jordan seven times."
   (vs. 10)

87

4. The dramatic results of unreserved obedience

"His flesh came again like unto the flesh of a little child." (vs. 14)

"He came up the sixth time no better, only much wetter. But the seventh time he was made whole," wrote John McNeill.

194. A SPIRITUAL CHECK-UP

"Is all well?" II Kings 5:21

1. Is all well respecting our past sins?
2. Is all well regarding our present peace?
3. Is all well with reference to our future hope?

195. THE VANQUISHING VISION

"And when the servant of the man of God was risen early, and gone forth, behold, an host compassed the city with horses and chariots. And his servant said unto him, Alas, my master! how shall we do? And he answered, Fear not: for they that be with us are more than they that be with them. And Elisha prayed, and said, Lord, I pray thee, open his eyes, that he may see. And the Lord opened the eyes of the young man; and he saw: and, behold, the mountain was full of horses and chariots of fire round about Elisha."

II Kings 6:15-17

1. The encircling circumstances
   (vs. 15)
2. The enabling consciousness
   (vs. 16)
3. The enduring conviction
   (vs. 17)

—R. G. Crawford

196. THE HIDDEN SACKCLOTH

"And it came to pass, when the king heard the words of the woman, that he rent his clothes; and he passed by upon the wall, and the people looked, and, behold, he had sackcloth within upon his flesh." II Kings 6:30

1. The text teaches us a lesson of restraint.
   Jehoram wore his sackcloth "within."
2. The text teaches us a lesson of contentment.
   The king as well as the people wore sackcloth.
3. The text teaches us a lesson of sympathy.
   We should be much more considerate to
   people if we only knew the sackcloth that
   they wear "within."
4. The text teaches a lesson of hope.
   The king's sackcloth was worn as a result
   of his sin. But he humbled himself before God, and God had mercy upon him
   and upon the city.

   —W. L. Watkinson, *The Blind Spot*

197. THE LAST VENTURE

"And there were four leprous men at the entering
in of the gate: and they said one to another, Why
sit we here until we die?"   II KINGS 7:3

We too must make such a venture:

1. In our work for God.
2. In the life of prayer.
3. In the life of faith.

—Henry Bett

198. EVERY CHRISTIAN A WITNESS

"They said one to another, We do not well: this
day is a day of good tidings, and we hold our
peace: if we tarry till the morning light, some
mischief will come upon us: now therefore come,
that we may go and tell the king's household."

II KINGS 7:9

Here there is a recognition that:

1. Silence would be sin.
   To hold one's peace when deliverance has
   come to the soul is altogether wrong. The
   way for evil to flourish is for good to
   keep silent.
2. Salvation must be shared.
3. Speed is essential.

The time is short. We must evangelize now.

—R. G. Crawford

199. THE BORED MONEY CHEST

"Jehoiada the priest took a chest, and bored a hole in the lid of it, and set it beside the altar, on the right side as one cometh into the house of the Lord." II KINGS 12:9

This is probably the first collection box on record. It seems to have been very similar in design to those now commonly in use. We are all familiar with the chest with the hole in the lid.

Note:

1. Institutional religion always requires financial support.

   It is noteworthy that it was the priest and not the prophet who made the collection box. Prophetic religion can flourish in poverty, priestly religion needs money for its maintenance.

2. Such support, when given, has a religious significance and value.

   He "set it beside the altar."

3. Those who thus support the work of God enter the holy place "on the right side."

4. No priest must be permitted to exploit the generosity of the Lord's people either for the aggrandizement of a church building or for his own luxurious living.

   God is not glorified when a "rich" church is maintained at the cost of keeping its members poor.

200. THE LOST BIBLE

"And Hilkiah the high priest said unto Shaphan the scribe, I have found the Book of the Law in the house of the Lord." II KINGS 22:8-10

It was, of course, only a small fragment of the Bible that was here lost and recovered. Neverthe-

less, the whole Bible may be similarly mislaid.
Let us inquire how.

1. The Bible is lost when the preacher does not expound it.
2. The Bible is lost when the people do not study it.
3. The Bible is lost when the readers do not practice it.

But—the Book may be rediscovered!

I CHRONICLES

201. WATER FROM THE WELL OF BETHLEHEM

I Chron. 11:16-19

1. The wish
   "Oh that one would give me drink of the water of the well of Bethlehem."
   (vs. 17)
2. The water
   "Water out of the well of Bethlehem."
   (vs. 18)
3. The warriors
   "The three brake through the host."
   (vs. 18)
4. The worship
   "David would not drink of it, but poured it out to the Lord."   (vs. 18b)

202. PRIORITY JOB

"Then on that day David delivered first this psalm to thank the Lord." I Chron. 16:7

Why should we, like David, not on one day only but on every day, make thanksgiving to God our first duty?

91

1. Because there is so much to be grateful for.
2. Because gratitude is all we can offer in return for many of the divine benefits.
3. Because the more thankful we are, the more we shall receive at God's hand.

203. THE LOST CHORD OF CONTEMPORARY CHRISTIANITY

"And all the people said, Amen."

I CHRON. 16:36

Everyone knows Adelaide Anne Procter's wistful lines, beginning:

> Seated one day at the organ,
> I was weary and ill at ease,
> And my fingers wandered idly
> Over the noisy keys,

and how she lost that magnificent closing chord.

Has the Church of today lost its great Amen; and, if so, how may it recover it?

1. The Amen of affirmation
2. The Amen of confirmation
3. The Amen of resignation
4. The Amen of jubilation

204. THE ALTAR OF THE AWAKENED CONSCIENCE

"Grant me the place of this threshingfloor, that I may build therein an altar unto the Lord: thou shalt grant it me for the full price: that the plague may be stayed from the people."   I CHRON. 21:22

1. It was an altar prompted by a sense of divine goodness.

    "Give me the place of this threshingfloor"—a symbol of God's harvest bounty.

2. It was an altar built to meet the rights of God.

    "An altar unto the Lord."

3. It was an altar which called for self-sacrifice.

    "Thou shalt grant it me for the full price."

4. It was an altar which was to bestow a great blessing.

—E. T. Evans, *The Vision of Victory*

205. ON PREPARING ABUNDANTLY

"David prepared abundantly before his death."
I CHRON. 22:5

1. David prepared abundantly by concentrating on a lovely vision which God was pleased to honor.
2. David prepared abundantly by contributing as far as in him lay to the realization of the lovely vision.
3. David prepared abundantly by confessing the supremacy of the Word of God in the matter of sin.

—Robert Barr, *In Sweet Remembrance*

206. WHAT TO DO WITH YOURSELF

"And who then is willing to consecrate his service this day unto the Lord?" I CHRON. 29:5

1. "Know thyself," said Socrates.
2. "Hate thyself," said Pascal.
3. "Consecrate thyself," says the Bible.

207. CONSECRATION

"Who then is willing to consecrate his service this day unto the Lord?" I CHRON. 29:5

According to this text, true consecration is:

1. Personal in its response.
   "Who"
2. Optional in its offer.
   "Is willing"
3. Practical in its expression.
   "His service"
4. Spiritual in its motive.
   "Unto the Lord"

208. CHRISTIAN CONSECRATION

"Who then is willing to consecrate his service this day unto the Lord?" I CHRON. 29:5

1. It is a personal thing.
   "Who then is willing?"
2. It is a practical thing.
   "His service"
3. It is a present thing.
   "This day"
4. It is a privileged thing.
   "Unto the Lord"

II CHRONICLES

209. LIFE'S WIDEST HORIZON

"And God said to Solomon, Because this was in thine heart, and thou hast not asked riches, wealth, or honour, nor the life of thine enemies, neither yet hast asked long life; but hast asked wisdom and knowledge for thyself, that thou mayest judge my people, over whom I have made thee king: Wisdom and knowledge is granted unto thee; and I will give thee riches, and wealth, and honour, such as none of the kings have had that have been before thee, neither shall there any after thee have the like." II Chron. 1:11-12.

1. Here we find a roadway whose signpost bears the inscription: "This way to long life."
2. Here we find a further roadway whose signpost bears the inscription: "This way to a career of struggle and victory."
3. Here we find, yet again, a roadway whose signpost bears the inscription: "This way to fame and honor."
4. Here, once more, we find a roadway whose signpost bears the inscription: "This way to a career of wealth and riches."

5. Here, finally, we find a roadway whose sign-post bears the inscription: "This way to wisdom and knowledge."

—Charles Frederick Wishart,
The God of the Unexpected

210. THE STORY OF A LIFE

"*Amasiah, . . . who willingly offered himself unto the Lord.*" II CHRON. 17:16

This man's cheerful consecration of himself to the Lord influenced two hundred thousand of his fellows to do likewise.

Observe:

1. What he did.
   "Offered himself"
2. How he did it.
   "Willingly"
3. Why he did it.
   "To the Lord"

—M. B. Tanner

211. SHIPWRECK

"*And after this did Jehoshaphat king of Judah join himself with Ahaziah king of Israel, who did very wickedly: And he joined himself with him to make ships. . . . And the ships were broken.*"
II CHRON. 20:35-37

Here we have:

1. A good man's secular failure.
2. A good man's secular failure through the intervention of God.
3. A good man's secular failure through the intervention of God resulting in spiritual gain.

—B. D. Johns

212. THE TEMPTATION OF SUCCESS

"*He was marvellously helped, till he was strong.*"
II CHRON. 26:15

The obvious lesson of Uzziah's life is the temptation of success or the danger of spiritual pride.

Pride has many forms.

    a. Material pride
    b. Hereditary pride
    c. Spiritual pride

Why is spiritual pride one of the most serious hindrances to the religious life?

1. Because it destroys in a man's heart that sense of divine need which is the root of all religion.
2. Because it is fatal to true prayer.
3. Because it stumbles at the Cross

      —W. Mackintosh Mackay,
        Problems in Living

213. WORSE THAN THE HEATHEN

"So Manasseh made Judah and the inhabitants of Jerusalem to err, and to do worse than the heathen, whom the Lord had destroyed before the children of Israel." II Chron. 33:9

"Worse than the heathen." Yes, this is the penalty of rejecting the fuller light: you sink lower than those who never had the light. It is possible to become worse than the heathen:

1. In faith and worship
2. In hope
3. In character
4. In happiness
5. In destiny

      —W. L. Watkinson

214. MEDDLING WITH GOD

"Forbear thee from meddling with God."
          II Chron. 35:21

1. We meddle with God when we criticize his ordering of the world.
2. We meddle with God when we interfere with his plan of salvation.
3. We meddle with God when we intrude upon his dealings in the lives of others.

4. We meddle with God when we limit the field of evangelism.

—George Johnstone Jeffrey

EZRA

215. HOW TO WORK FOR GOD

"The people gathered themselves together as one man to Jerusalem . . . and builded the altar of the God of Israel, . . . and offered the daily burnt offerings by number, according to the custom, as the duty of every day required." Ezra 3:1-4

Such service is marked by:

1. Unity of effort
   "As one man."
2. Loyalty to law
   "According to the custom."
3. Wise apportionment
   "As the day required."

216. PREPAREDNESS OF HEART

"For Ezra had prepared his heart to seek the law of the Lord, and to do it, and to teach in Israel statutes and judgments." Ezra 7:10

1. Ezra prepared.
2. Ezra prepared his heart.
3. Ezra prepared his heart to seek the law of the Lord, and to do it.
4. Ezra prepared his heart to teach the law of the Lord of Israel.

NEHEMIAH

217. RIDING ROUND THE RUINS
NEH. 2:12-18

Here is a vivid little narrative—the prophet riding on horseback in the moonlight round the ruined city. We can see it all in our mind's eye as if we had been there.

Four phrases may help us to unfold the breathless tale.

1. The returned exile
2. The midnight survey
3. The ruined splendor
    Sad sight after the war: Spurgeon's Tabernacle, Whitefield's Tabernacle, Parker's City Temple, Alexander Maclaren's Union Chapel, Manchester—all laid waste.
4. The resolve to rebuild

218. PREOCCUPIED
"*I am doing a great work, so that I cannot come down.*" NEH. 6:3

Some lessons are here which I will ask you to ponder:

1. Here is a rebuke to false humility.
2. Here is the true defense against temptation.
3. Here is the right answer to suggestions of spiritual compromise.

—Hugh Ross Mackintosh, *Sermons*

219. SELF-RESPECT
"*And I said, Should such a man as I flee? and who is there, that, being as I am, would go into the temple to save his life? I will not go in.*"
NEH. 6:11

Consider:

1. The nature of self-respect
    a) It is not pride.
    b) It is not selfishness.

2. The grounds of self-respect
   It springs from the consciousness that we have:
   a) A great nature and must duly honor it.
   b) A great name, and must live up to it.
   c) A great work to do and must get down to it.

3. The value of self-respect
   a) It has guiding value.
   b) It has inspiring value.
   c) It has social value—example.
   d) It has personal value—satisfaction.

—W. L. Watkinson

220. THE SPIRIT OF CHRISTMAS

"Then he [Nehemiah] said unto them, Go your way, eat the fat, and drink the sweet, and send portions unto them for whom nothing is prepared: for this day is holy unto our Lord."

NEH. 8:10-12

Here we find:

1. Gaiety
   "Eat the fat, and drink the sweet."

2. Generosity
   "Send portions."

3. Godliness
   "For this day is holy."

—C. Leslie Brewer

221. ON BEING SECOND

"Bakbukiah the second among his brethren."

NEH. 11:17

Someone has said that the most difficult business of life is to learn to take second place gracefully. That is certainly true of an ambitious person, though some seem to prefer second place because it involves less publicity and less responsibility.

1. It is easier to be a good first than a good second.

99

2. It is better to be a good second than a poor first.
3. It is good seconds that make good firsts what they are.

> It takes more skill than tongue can tell
> To play the second fiddle well.

ESTHER

222. FOUR BANQUETS IN THE BOOK OF ESTHER

1. The banquet of deposition
   Esth. 1:3
2. The banquet of coronation
   Esth. 2:18
3. The banquet of petition
   Esth. 5:4-8
4. The banquet of commemoration
   Esth. 9:17

223. THE TRANSFIGURED SACKCLOTH

"For none might enter into the king's gate clothed with sackcloth." Esth. 4:2

The sign of affliction was thus excluded from the Persian court in order that royalty might not be discomposed. This disposition to place an interdict on disagreeable things still survives.

Not, however, in Christianity.

1. The sackcloth of sin
   Christianity takes the full measure of that.
   Christ recognizes sin as a doctor diagnoses disease in order to destroy it.
2. The sackcloth of sorrow
   Christianity takes the full measure of that.
   So far from shutting his gate on the sackcloth, Christ adopted it, and showed how it might become a robe of glory.

3. The sackcloth of death

Christianity takes the full measure of that. Without evasion or euphony Christ recognizes the somber mystery. He himself submitted to death, but of his death he made a glorious triumph.

—W. L. Watkinson,
The Transfigured Sackcloth

224. FOR SUCH A TIME AS THIS

"Who knoweth whether thou art come to the kingdom for such a time as this?" Esth. 4:14

Here we have presented to us a drama in four scenes:

1. Scene One: On the housetops of the Jewish homes.

Men and women kneeling with uplifted eyes and hands pressed together. They have learned of their impending doom and are praying to their God.

2. Scene Two: The open square beneath the Queen's window.

Mordecai summons her to the lattice.

3. Scene Three: The Queen's apartments.

Three days she has been fasting and pray-to God. The hour is come for her to venture uninvited into the royal presence.

4. Scene Four: The banquet hall.

King and courtiers have been feasting many days. Esther enters. Will the sceptre be extended to her? It is. "What wilt thou, queen Esther? and what is thy request? it shall be even given thee to the half of the kingdom." The crisis is averted. God's people are spared.

—David James Burrell,
Wayfarers of the Bible

225. UNREST WITHIN

"Yet all this availeth me nothing, so long as I see Mordecai the Jew sitting at the king's gate." Esth. 5:13

1. No outward good can meet an inward need.
2. An inward evil can mar any outward good.
3. The highest blessing is a holy heart.

—Arthur T. Pierson, *The Making of a Sermon*

JOB

226. HEDGED

"Hast not thou made an hedge about him, and about his house, and about all that he hath on every side?" JOB 1:10

There are just two things I want to speak about:

1. The hedge

What does that speak of?

a) Proprietorship?
b) Preciousness?
c) Protection?
d) Purpose?

2. The hedged

Very briefly let me suggest two or three things that ought to characterize the hedged life.

a) Separation.
b) Fruitfulness
c) Beauty
d) Patience

—W. W. Weeks, *The Face of Christ*

227. DESPAIR AND FAITH

"Curse God, and die." JOB 2:9
"Hope thou in God." Ps. 42:11

Two contrasted moods toward life, the world and the universe have in all ages contended for empire over the mind of man. These two moods are despair and faith, pessimism and hope.

1. These two moods are contrasted as vision.
   Pessimism sees only the evil; faith sees
   both the evil and the good.
2. These two moods are contrasted in action.
   Pessimism, in so far as it is logical, is
   impotence; faith is power.
3. These two moods are contrasted in issue.
   Pessimism is unproductive; faith is marked
   by achievement.
   —George A. Gordon, *Voices of the Age*

228. SUPPORTING WORDS

"*Your words have kept men on their feet.*"

Job 4:4 Moffatt

1. Men are meant to be on their feet.
2. There is much in life which tends to sweep
   them off their feet.
3. When that happens, there is nothing like
   the words of a man who knows God at first-
   hand for enabling men to maintain a moral
   stand.

229. SILENCE—AND A VOICE

(Remembrance Day Sermon Outline)
"*There was silence, and I heard a voice.*"

Job 4:16

Silence, and then a voice! How characteristic that
is of the supreme moments in spiritual history.
What is the voice that speaks in the silence of
Armistice Day?

1. It is the voice of the past, the voice of
   memory.
2. It is the voice of sacrifice.
3. It is the voice of duty.

—Stuart W. McWilliam, *Expository Times*

230. NOT BY BREAD ALONE

"*Doth the wild ass bray when he hath grass? or
loweth the ox over his fodder?*"   Job 6:5

1. Grass, or fodder, is for beasts not only the
   means of life, but also the meaning of life.

2. Man needs more than food.
3. If existence is to have meaning for him, he needs likewise the bread of life, which is Jesus.

—Neville Davis

231. THE LOOM OF LIFE

"My days are swifter than a weaver's shuttle."

Job 7:6

1. Our days are swift.
2. Each day adds a thread to the web of life.
3. What we weave in time, we wear in eternity.

—Unknown

232. THE RUSH AND THE MIRE

"Can the rush grow up without mire?" Job 8:11

1. At the outset we must admit the mighty constraining influence of one's surroundings.
2. The influence of surroundings is not the *deciding* influence in life.
3. Surroundings can be transformed by the vital principle.

—Walter Merle Smith,
Giving a Man Another Chance

233. A SPIDER'S WEB

"Whose trust is a spider's web." Job 8:14

Here is a graphic figure, a picture of the false trust of those who forget God. It is, says Bildad, "a spider's web." How apt is the metaphor! For consider:

1. A spider's web is self-derived.
2. A spider's web is frail.
3. A spider's web entangles to destroy.

234. POSTING THROUGH LIFE

"My days are swifter than a post." Job 9:25

1. Our days are like a post because they carry a message.

2. Our days are like a post because they are always in transit.
3. Our days are like a post because they have a destination.

235. THE BREVITY OF HUMAN LIFE

"Now my days are swifter than a post: they flee away, they see no good. They are passed away as the swift ships." JOB 9:25-26

How do our days pass away like ships?

1. They pass quickly because they are going to a goal.
2. They pass quickly because there is no safe anchorage in mid-ocean.
3. They pass quickly, like swift ships, because that is the will of the captain.

236. NO INFERIORITY COMPLEX

"I am not inferior to you." JOB 12:3

A buoyant young man once said to me: "I don't believe in feeling inferior." Evidently Job was of the same mind. Note that the consciousness of superiority may arise from various things:

1. Superiority of natural endowment
2. Superiority of social preferment
3. Superiority of practical achievement
4. Superiority of intellectual enlightenment
5. Superiority of spiritual enrichment

Incomparably the greatest of these is the last.

237. A QUESTION THAT HAUNTS THE HEART

"If a man die, shall he live again?" JOB 14:14

Some time ago a great London newspaper had a striking series of articles on "Where are the dead?" Leading scientists, thinkers and novelists were asked to give their views. Whether they really helped the sorrowing heart is a matter of doubt, but they did send up the circulation of the paper. The question "Where are the dead?" proved to be good copy because there are bleeding and broken hearts everywhere, which hunger for the hope, the comfort, and the assurance of immortality.

Three books suggest an answer to Job's interrogation.

1. There is the book of nature.
    Here we see life conquering death.
2. There is the book of human life.
    Here we find love defying death.
3. There is the book of revelation.
    Here we discover Christ destroying death.

—Samuel Chadwick

238. THE LAST CHANGE
"Till my change come." Job 14:14

1. It might have been an unwelcome change.
2. It will be a great change.
3. It may be a sudden change.
4. It is likely to be an unattended change.
5. It must be a final change.

—R. Andrew Griffin

239. IF A MAN DIE?
"If a man die, shall he live again?" Job 14:14
There are, broadly speaking, four answers to this question.

1. Materialism says, "No."
2. Agnosticism says, "I don't know."
3. Spiritualism says, "Only a part of him survives."
4. Christianity says, "For weal or woe, his whole personality will live again and that for ever."

240. THE CONSOLATIONS OF GOD
"Are the consolations of God small with thee?"
                                        Job 15:11

What are those consolations?

1. The consolation of his presence

2. The consolation of forgiveness
3. The consolation of heaven

—C. A. Stephens

241. THE PROFIT OF PRAYER

"What profit should we have, if we pray?"

Job 21:15

1. The profit of self-mastery
2. The profit of social influence
3. The profit of spiritual communion
4. The profit of adequate resources

242. THE PROFIT OF PRAYER

"What profit should we have, if we pray?"

Job 21:15

The profit of prayer consists largely of three things:

1. Forgiveness for life's failures
2. Adequacy to life's demands
3. Harmony in life's relationships

243. THE PROFIT OF PRAYER

"What profit should we have, if we pray?"

Job 21:15

Years ago, a train on which I was traveling halted for some time outside Shrewsbury Station. Opposite me in the compartment were two little boys. One had his nose glued to the glass of the window and was staring out impatiently; the other was tinkering with the button of the bell one rings to summon the attendant. After standing for several minutes, the train suddenly began to move. "Hurrah!" shouted the first little fellow, "We're off!" "Of course," said the other, "didn't you see me press the button?"

Some people would try to persuade us that there is no more real relation between our prayers and what happens in the world than between the pressing of that button and the movement of the train. Echoing our text, they want to ask:

107

"What profit should we have, if we pray?" Let us provide them with five answers.

1. Prayer is profitable because it makes God realizable.
2. Prayer is profitable because it makes sin impossible.
3. Prayer is profitable because it makes self manageable.
4. Prayer is profitable because it makes truth cognizable.
5. Prayer is profitable because it makes power available.

244. PROFITABLE PRAYER

"What profit should we have, if we pray?"

Job 21:15

1. Prayer brings the right perspective on life's problems.
2. Prayer provides an opportunity for honest self-criticism.
    "Prayer-time is God's punishment-time" (F. W. Faber).
3. Prayer puts the soul in touch with infinite resources.

245. MAKING GOD'S ACQUAINTANCE

"Acquaint now thyself with him, and be at peace."

Job 22:21

1. What to do
    "Acquaint"
2. When to do it
    "Now"
3. Who should do it
    "Thyself"
4. Why do it?
    "Be at peace"

—Unknown

246. FINDING GOD

"Oh that I knew where I might find him!"

Job 23:3

This ancient cry finds an echo in many hearts

today. What answer shall we give to it? We can say that God is to be found in nature, in history, and in the Bible. Or we can come closer and say that God can be discovered in the depths of a man's own life. Thus:

1. You will find him beyond the confession of personal moral failure and a plea for pardon.
2. You will find him beyond the righting of wrong relationships.
3. You will find him beyond the acceptance of each daunting challenge.
4. You will find him beyond the doing of some difficult duty.
5. You will find him supremely in the exercise of private prayer.

247. IN QUEST OF THE DIVINE

"Oh, that I knew where I might find him! that I might even come unto his seat." JOB 23:3

Here we have:

1. The language of painful separation.
2. The language of conscious loss.
3. The language of passionate desire.

—Unknown

248. REMOVING THE LANDMARKS

"Some remove the landmarks." JOB 24:2

1. Some remove the landmarks of the historic creed.
2. Some remove the landmarks of Christian morality.
3. Some remove the landmarks of public worship.

    In Britain, churches have been turned into warehouses, garages, and at least one into a zoo!

249. THE MINISTRY OF INTERRUPTION

"He divideth the sea with his power."

JOB 26:12

Think, to begin with, of some familiar interruptions

a) The interruption of night
b) The interruption of suffering
c) The interruption of the grave

Now note that:

1. By the ministry of interruption, God wakens us to the value of time.
2. By the ministry of interruption, God checks the force of evil in the world.
3. By the ministry of interruption, God imparts a certain charm to life.
4. By the ministry of interruption, God shows us there are larger plans than ours.

—G. H. Morrison, *The Incomparable Christ*

250. THE UNGUESSED WAY

"*There is a path which no fowl knoweth, and which the vulture's eye hath not seen.*"

Job 28:7

Migratory birds have tracks unknown to man which they pursue with unwearied regularity year by year; but man has ways which the birds may search for in vain, no matter how keen their eye or distant their vision.

1. Man has paths which fowls have not guessed and ways that they have not seen.
2. God can lead us as he can never guide fowls.
3. The direction of some of these divine paths may be indicated.
   a) There is the way of elective love.
   b) There is the way of approach to Christ.
   c) There is the way of God's thinking.
   d) There is the way of God's chastening.
   e) There is the way of the spirit leaping free at death.

—W. Y. Fullerton, *God's Highway*

251. THE DEAR DEAD DISTANT DAYS

"*When my children were about me.*"

Job 29:5

1. It is well for parents to have their children
   as much about them as possible.
2. Though parents do their best to have their
   children about them, the children will not
   be there long.
3. As parents, we should so deal with our
   children that, when they are no longer about
   us, we need not look back with misgiving.

   —Thomas Davies, *Sermonic Studies*

252. AN OPTICAL COVENANT

"*I made a covenant with mine eyes.*"   JOB 31:1
This is part of Job's eloquent apologia. He tells
us here that he has made a pact with his eyes.
What did that comprise? It meant a resolve:

1. Not to look desiringly on evil.
2. Not to look expressing evil.
3. Not to look condoning evil.

253. THE VALUE OF LIFE

"*The Spirit of God hath made me, and the breath
of the Almighty hath given me life.*"   JOB 33:4

1. Life in its origin is infinitely important.
2. Human life is precious from the services
   it may render to God in the advancement
   of his glory.
3. Life is infinitely valuable because of the
   eternal consequences flowing from it.

   —Theodore Cuyler

254. THE PROFITS OF RELIGION

"*What profit shall I have, if I be cleansed from
my sin?*"   JOB 35:3
"*What profit should we have, if we pray unto
him?*"   JOB 21:15
"*What profit is it that we have kept His ordinance,
and that we have walked mournfully before the
Lord of hosts?*"   MAL. 3:14

These cynical questions suggest their own answers.
In true religion there is:

1. The profit of a life purged of its past.
2. The profit of a life reinforced by sufficient resources.
3. The profit of a life rightly related to law.

255. SONGS IN THE NIGHT

"But none saith, Where is God, my maker, who giveth songs in the night?" JOB 35:10

1. God gives, in the night of sin, the song of salvation.
2. God gives, in the night of sorrow, the song of consolation.
3. God gives, in the night of mystery, the song of revelation.

256. THE TREASURES OF THE SNOW

"Hast thou entered into the treasures of the snow?" JOB 38:22

1. Snow beautifies
2. Snow purifies
3. Snow pacifies
4. Snow fructifies

PSALMS

257. THE PSALM OF THE TWO WAYS

Ps. 1

1. The way that prospers
   a) Defined
      (1) negatively—vs. 1
      (2) positively—vs. 2
   b) Described—"like a tree"
      (1) firm—"planted"
      (2) fruitful—"bringeth forth his fruit."

(3) flourishing—"his leaf also shall not wither."

2. The way that perishes
   a) Not "walk"—driven "like chaff."
   b) Not stand in judgment.
   c) Not sit in congregation of righteous.
                     —Unknown

258. THE PROGRAMME OF EVIL

"Blessed is the man that walketh not in the counsel of the ungodly, nor standeth in the way of sinners, nor sitteth in the seat of the scornful."
                     Ps. 1:1

1. "Walketh"
2. "Standeth"
3. "Sitteth"

Result: "The way of the ungodly shall perish."
              —W. L. Watkinson

259. PLANTED LIKE A TREE

"He shall be like a tree planted by the rivers of water." Ps. 1:3

Note:

1. Trees do not plant themselves.
2. Trees do not support themselves.
3. Trees do not bear fruit for themselves.
                     —Unknown

260. THE THREE SELAHS
Ps. 3

The term "selah" may perhaps be Englished "pause and ponder."

1. The selah of a false insinuation
    "Many there be which say of my soul, There is no help for him in God. Selah."
                   (vs. 2)
2. The selah of a favored supplication
    "I cried unto the Lord with my voice, and he heard me out of his holy hill. Selah."
                   (vs. 4)
3. The selah of a full salvation
    "Salvation belongeth unto the Lord: thy

blessing is upon thy people. Selah."
(vs. 8)

261. ENLARGEMENT IN DISTRESS

"Thou hast enlarged me when I was in distress."
Ps. 4:1

Through distress there can come:

1. An enlargement of personal character
2. An enlargement of personal influence
3. An enlargement of personal experience with God

—John C. Lambert, *The Omnipotent Cross*

262. WHAT PRAYER IS

"In the morning will I direct my prayer unto thee, and will look up." Ps. 5:3

1. Prayer is a sin killer.
   You will either have to give up sinning or give up praying.
2. Prayer is a power bringer.
   It is the hand that touches Christ's garment and causes his divine life to flow into us.
3. Prayer is a victory giver.
   Bunyan found that it could wound and defeat the enemy.
4. Prayer is a holiness producer.
   As Moses communed with God, his face commenced to shine.
5. Prayer is an obstacle remover.
   Prayer unlocked the iron gate of Peter's prison.
6. Prayer is a Christ revealer.
   It clears our vision and enables us to see things in their true proportions, and also to perceive that the invisible hosts of God are with us.

—M. B. Tanner

263. THE SAPPER

"He made a pit, and digged it and is fallen into the ditch which he made." Ps. 7:15

1. How this sapping may be done.
    a) By lowering a man's reputation
    b) By sapping his business
    c) By endangering his character
2. What this sapping really is.
    a) Dark work
    b) Dirty work
    c) Dismal work
    d) Degrading work

—W. L. Watkinson

264. THE ABSURDITY OF ATHEISM

"The fool hath said in his heart, There is no God." Ps. 14:1

That atheism is absurd is proved:

1. By its assertion that creation is without a cause.
2. By its contradiction of the universal consciousness of men.
3. By its being the utterance only of the heart (not of the judgment) even of fools.

—Daniel P. Kidder, Homiletics

265. THE FOOL'S CREED

"The fool hath said in his heart, There is no God." Ps. 14:1

In these days when for the first time in history atheism has become militant and is challenging the basic axiom of the Christian faith, it may be well for us to remind ourselves of the folly of such materialist philosophy.

What does it do?

1. It leaves creation without a Creator.
2. It leaves design without a designer.
3. It leaves the universe without a controller.
4. It leaves human history without a ruler.
5. It leaves morality without any basis of authority.
6. It leaves sin without any adequate restraint.

115

7. It leaves death without any hope or here-after.

—A. T. Pierson, *The Making of a Sermon*

266. THREE FOOLS

1. The atheistic fool
   "The fool hath said in his heart, There is no God." Ps. 14:1
2. The materialistic fool
   "Thou fool, this night thy soul shall be required of thee." Luke 12:20
3. The altruistic fool
   "We are fools for Christ's sake."
   I Cor. 4:10

267. THE HEAVENLY CITIZEN

"Lord, who shall abide in thy tabernacle? who shall dwell in thy holy hill?" Ps. 15:1

As we study this brief and wonderful psalm we find ourselves looking at a picture of a true citizen of Zion. What is he like? To that question the rest of the psalm provides an answer.

1. The heavenly citizen is one whose life is blameless.
   "He that walketh uprightly, and worketh righteousness, and speaketh truth in his heart." (vs. 2)
2. The heavenly citizen is one who is charitable towards his neighbor.
   "He that slandereth not with his tongue, nor doeth evil to his neighbor, nor taketh up a reproach against his neighbor." (vs. 3)
3. The heavenly citizen is one who is careful of his friendships.
   "In whose eyes a vile person is condemned; but he honoureth them that fear the Lord." (vs. 4a, b)
4. The heavenly citizen is one whose word is his bond.

"He that sweareth to his own hurt, and changeth not." (vs. 4c, d)

5. The heavenly citizen is one who is merciful in his dealings.

"He that putteth not out his money to usury, nor taketh reward against the innocent." (vs. 5a)

Note result: "He that doeth these things shall never be moved." (vs. 5b)

—Unknown

268. THE BLESSEDNESS OF THE RIGHTEOUS

"As for me, I will behold thy face in righteousness. I shall be satisfied, when I awake, with thy likeness." Ps. 17:15

Consider the nature of this blessedness:

1. The vision of the face of God
2. The soul's participation in His likeness
3. The resulting satisfaction

—John Howe

269. FOUR SOUNDS

1. The sound of creation
   "Their line is gone out through all the earth." Ps. 19:4
2. The sound of salvation
   "Blessed is the people that know the joyful sound." Ps. 89:15
3. The sound of proclamation
   "From you sounded out the word of the Lord." I Thess. 1:8
4. The sound of translation
   "The trumpet shall sound."

I Cor. 15:52

270. GOD'S LAW IS NOT "ON APPROVAL"

"The law of the Lord is perfect, converting the soul." Ps. 19:7

1. Some laws apply only to those who accept them—

117

The law of God is for all.

2. Some laws apply exclusively to certain localities—
    The law of God is binding everywhere.

3. Some laws alter with the passing of time—
    The law of God stands forever.

—W. E. Sangster, *Westminster Sermons* (Vol. I)

271. CONCERNING THE COMMANDMENTS
Ps. 19:7-11

The Psalmist says of the Commandments:

1. They are powerful
    "Converting the soul." (vs. 7)
2. They are plain
    "Making wise the simple." (vs. 7)
3. They are pleasing
    "Rejoicing the heart." (vs. 8)
4. They are pure
    "The commandment of the Lord is pure."
    (vs. 8)
5. They are permanent
    "Enduring for ever." (vs. 9)
6. They are precious
    "More desirable than much fine gold."
    (vs. 10)
7. They are preventive
    "By them is thy servant warned."
    (vs. 11)

—Unknown

272. THE SIN OF SELF-CONFIDENCE

"*Keep back thy servant also from presumptuous sins; let them not have dominion over me: then shall I be upright, and I shall be innocent from great transgression.*" Ps. 19:13

What is it to be guilty of presumptuous sin?

1. To treat negligently our secret faults
2. To despise the beginnings of habit
3. To expose ourselves unnecessarily to temptation

4. To encounter the inevitable perils of life
without due preparation
—W. L. Watkinson, *The Fatal Barter*

273. TRILOGY

1. The psalm of the cross
—Ps. 22
2. The psalm of the crook
—Ps. 23
3. The psalm of the crown
—Ps. 24

274. WHEN NO ANSWER SEEMS TO COME

"*Why art thou so far from helping me?*"

Ps. 22:1

W. Y. Fullerton once observed that there are
two doors into the full blessing of the gospel.
Over one is written the word "whosoever." "Whosoever will, let him come." Over the other is inscribed: "Whatsoever." "Whatsoever ye shall ask
in my name, I will do it."

This last is a prodigious promise. Is it true? Do
we always get an answer to our prayers?

1. We must ever be careful to distinguish between denial and delay.
2. We must never forget that negative answers
are answers just as real as positive ones.
3. We must always recognize that God's replies to our requests may be very different
from what we anticipate.

275. WORM'S EYE VIEW

"*But I am a worm, and no man.*" Ps. 22:6

What sort of suffering does this somber sentence
describe?

1. It speaks of ignorant suffering.
A worm is blind.
2. It speaks of innocent suffering.
A worm can do no wrong to deserve it.

119

3. It speaks of impotent suffering.
Most creatures have been furnished by
nature with some means of self-protection
—fight or flight. But a worm can neither
fight nor fly. It can only suffer. "Even
a worm will turn," they say. But no one
has ever seen a worm doing it!

276. THE PSALM OF LIFE

Ps. 23

A young preacher is said to have begun a sermon
on the twenty-third psalm with the words: "This
psalm is written from the point of view of a
sheep!" Aside from the naïveté of the remark, it
is not really true. A sheep would look more than
odd sitting at a table!   (vs. 5)

The best definition of the psalm I know is this:
"A mirror of life lived with God."

There are three strophes in it. Taking them in
turn, we see:
1. The shepherd and the sheep   (vss. 1, 2)
2. The guide and the traveller   (vss. 3, 4)
3. The host and the guest   (vss. 5, 6)

—W. Graham Scroggie

277. IN AND OUT

Ps. 23

John 10

The twenty-third psalm and the tenth chapter of
John are antiphonal. Out of the valley of the
shadow of death the Psalmist called, "The Lord
is my shepherd," and back from the sunny hillside
of the Gospel comes the answer of Jesus, "I am
the good shepherd."

Because Christ is the good shepherd we shall go
in and out and find pasture.
1. First we must learn the principle of alterna-
tion between the going in to the shelter
of the Christian faith and out to the exposure of it.

2. Secondly, the Christian must alternate between going in to the restraints of his religion and going out to the liberties of it.
3. Thirdly, the Christian shall go in to the close-up views of the sheepfold and shall go out to the long vistas of the pasture.

—Ralph W. Sockman,
The Unemployed Carpenter

278. THE EARTH IS THE LORD'S

"The earth is the Lord's and the fullness thereof."
Ps. 24:1

What is the significance of this assertion?
1. First of all, it furnishes a rebuke to man's pride and self-sufficiency.
2. In the second place, it is a rebuke to man's ingratitude.
3. Finally, it is a rebuke to man's selfishness

—John B. Nettleship

279. ASCENDING THE HILL OF THE LORD

"Who shall ascend the hill of the Lord? or who shall stand in his holy place?" Ps. 24:3

When Dante begins to make the real ascent to Paradise he has to mount three steps at the beginning of the journey. There is first a step of white marble. Then there is a step which is rough, broken and uneven. And, third, there is a step of flaming red porphyry.

If we wish to ascend the hill of the Lord, these are the first three steps which set us on the road:
1. We begin with the step of white marble.
    It is the symbol of purity and sincerity.
2. From the white marble we pass to the rough and broken step.
    It is the broken and contrite heart.
3. Then we reach the third step of the flaming red porphyry.
    This is the kindling of love, the red glow of sacrificial affection.

—John Henry Jowett

280. ON THE SLOPE

"Who shall ascend into the hill of the Lord?"

Ps. 24:3

We are all of us living on a slope. The one thing we cannot do is walk at our ease on the level. We must either ascend or descend. Suppose we got that truth firmly into our minds, what results would issue?

1. A wholesome sense of insecurity
2. A realization that it is impossible to stand still
3. A conviction that there is no growth in goodness without struggle and strain

—J. D. Jones, *The Gospel of the Sovereignty*

281. THE LORD'S LEISURE

"Tarry thou the Lord's leisure." Ps. 27:16

Book of Common Prayer

"The trouble is," remarked William Booth on one occasion, "the Lord is not in a hurry, and I am." That is the trouble with most of us. We need to take to heart the counsel of the text.

1. Tarry the Lord's leisure in the matter of the working out of confessed and repented sin.
2. Tarry the Lord's leisure in the matter of the issue of life's discipline.
3. Tarry the Lord's leisure in the matter of the unfolding of his plan.
4. Tarry the Lord's leisure in the matter of his answering of your prayers.
5. Tarry the Lord's leisure in the matter of the expression of his power in your experience.
6. Tarry the Lord's leisure in the matter of possible delays in the fruition of your work for him.

282. IS GOD DUMB?

"Be not silent to me." Ps. 28:1

1. God may be speaking, or willing to speak, when we cannot hear.

2. God may be speaking when we fail to recognize his voice.
3. If God is silent, and wants to be so, it is in order that we may walk by faith.

—B. Parker Willcox

283. THE SIGNIFICANCE OF A CRY

"*Hear the voice of my supplications, when I cry unto thee.*" Ps. 28:2

1. It intimates identity.
2. It presupposes pity.
3. It notifies need.
4. It secures supply.

> He makes the grass the hills adorn
> And clothes the smiling fields with corn;
> The beasts with food His hands supply
> And the young ravens when they cry.

—Isaac Watts

284. IN THY HAND

"*My times are in thy hand.*" Ps. 31:15

1. "In thy hand"—that means that they belong to thee.
2. "In thy hand"—that suggests that thou makest them a gift to me.
   "My" times but "thy" hand.
3. "In thy hand"—that implies that thou hast a grip of them.
4. "In thy hand"—that intimates that thou wilt guard them with thine omnipotence.

285. NO LANGUAGE BUT A CRY

"*This poor man cried, and the Lord heard him.*"
Ps. 34:6

Nearly every creature has its own distinctive cry. The wild call of the lonely lapwing; the muffled roar of the forest lion; the pathetic bleat of the fleecy little lamb.

Now, when you come to think of it, a cry is a

123

wonderful thing. It is enough in itself to prove that the world is not a mere machine, for whoever would dream of crying to a machine?

Consider four types of cry:

1. The cry of fear
2. The cry of need
3. The cry of love
4. The cry of conquest

286. THE GREAT EXPERIMENT

"O taste and see that the Lord is good: blessed is the man that trusteth in him." Ps. 34:8

While it is of importance that we should insist upon sound doctrine, we must also take care that we insist upon the necessity of a vital experience.

Note here:

1. The experiment
    "O taste and see."
2. The expression
    "The Lord is good."
3. The experience
    "Blessed is the man that trusteth in him."
                                   —M. B. Tanner

287. THE FOUNTAIN OF LIFE

"With thee is the fountain of life." Ps. 36:9

This fountain is:

1. Rich in its source.
2. Sovereign in its gift.
3. Exhaustless in its supply.
4. Continuous in its flow.
5. Fertilizing in its streams.

                                   —Unknown

288. THE PSYCHOLOGY OF TRUE PREACHING

1. Meditation
    "While I was musing."

2. Inspiration
   "The fire burned."
3. Ministration
   "Then spake I."
   Ps. 39:3

289. THE WHEREABOUTS OF GOD

"My tears have been my meat day and night, while they continually say unto me, Where is thy God?"
Ps. 42:3

That is a taunt terrible to bear—especially when, to be quite honest, you don't know the answer to the question which it poses! It is a taunt which we all hear:

1. In moments of personal crisis.
2. In moments of daunting doubt.
3. In moments of nervous depression.
4. In moments of challenge to the exercise of the supernatural.

290. HARMONIES

"Deep calleth unto deep." Ps. 42:7

1. Deeps respond to deeps.
   a) The deep of God's purposes has been answered by the deep of his providence.
   b) The deep of human sin has been responded to by the deep of Christ's atonement.
   c) The deep of human weakness has been responded to by the deep of God's almightiness.
2. Deeps that predict deeps.
   a) The deep desire for holiness which will one day be answered by the deep of perfect conformity to the divine will.
   b) The deep desire for fellowship with our departed friends which will one day have its perfect response in the glad reunion beyond the grave.
   c) The deep of an eternal loss that awaits

125

the deep of a final rejection of our Lord.

3. Deeps that call for answering deeps.
   a) The great deep of Christ's sacrifice for us calls for a corresponding deep of faith and confidence on your part and mine.
   b) The deep of human sin and sorrow is calling for a corresponding deep of sacrificial service.
   c) The deep yearning of the heart of Christ for fellowship with his people ought to have answering it a deep resolve on their part to be his only and his always.

—W. W. Weeks, *The Face of Christ*

291. THE RIVER OF GOD

"*There is a river, the streams whereof shall make glad the city of God.*" Ps. 46:4

It is no coincidence that so many of the world's great cities have been built on the banks of rivers —New York on the Hudson, London on the Thames, Paris on the Seine, and so on. Jerusalem has no river. Yet the Psalmist says that it has— the river of a pure, spiritual religion.

1. A river provides supply.
2. A river promotes purity.
3. A river fosters fertility.
4. A river denotes division.
5. A river means movement.
6. A river connotes continuity.
7. A river suggests navigation.

292. HOW TO KNOW GOD

"*Be still, and know that I am God.*"

Ps. 46:10

Here are the possibilities:

1. "Be startled, and fear that I am God."
2. "Be stirred, and feel that I am God."
3. "Be still, and know that I am God."

293. THE SCHOOL OF SILENCE

"Be still, and know that I am God." Ps. 46:10

There is a double action in the text. It is retro-active. Be still and you shall know. On the other hand, know and you shall be still.

1. There is the school of silence which we call sleep.
2. There is the school of silence which is called the Sabbath.
3. There is the school of silence which we call sorrow.

—Hugh T. Kerr, *The Highway of Life*

294. ONE MAN'S VIEW OF GOD

"God is known in her palaces for a refuge."
Ps. 48:3

1. The reality of God
   "God is."
2. The revelation of God
   "God is known."
3. The region where the revelation is made
   "God is known in her palaces."
4. The refuge which, to those who rightly seek it, is always found in God's reality.
   "God is known in her palaces for a refuge."

Adapted.
—William Arnot

295. SEEING THE SIGHTS OF THE CITY

"Walk about Zion, and go round about her: tell the towers thereof. Mark ye well her bulwarks, consider her palaces; that ye may tell it to the generation following." Ps. 48:12-13

This passage suggests three thoughts concerning the church of God.

1. The church of God invites inspection.
   It has nothing to hide and so challenges investigation. "Walk about Zion."
2. The church of God offers a refuge.

127

"Tell the towers thereof. Mark ye well her bulwarks, consider her palaces."

3. The church of God makes history.

"That ye may tell it to the generation following."

—Daniel Hughes, *The Making of Man*

296. DARK SAYINGS ON THE HARP

"I will open my dark saying upon the harp."

Ps. 49:4

1. The dark saying of sin and the harp of forgiveness
2. The dark saying of doubt and the harp of faith
3. The dark saying of suffering and the harp of sympathy
4. The dark saying of death and the harp of immortality

297. THE STUFF THAT WEIGHS UPON THE HEART

"My sin is ever before me." Ps. 51:3

There is:

1. A "my" attached to sin.

I cannot, like Adam, distribute the blame for sin to anyone else. My only hope is to say with David, "I acknowledge my transgressions."

2. A memory attached to sin.

It is ever before me, and only the cleansing of Christ can remove that memory.

3. A misery attached to sin.

Sin fascinates and then assassinates.

—R. G. Crawford

298. WHITER THAN SNOW

"Wash me, and I shall be whiter than snow."

Ps. 51:7

Picture Alexander Whyte, dazzled by the winter sunshine on the Scottish mountains, crying:

"Wash me, and I shall be whiter than snow!"
1. Snow is unrivaled in its purity.
2. Snow is beautiful as a covering.
3. Snow is startling in its challenge.
4. Snow is easily soiled.

299. THE PRAYER FOR A CLEAN HEART

"*Create in me a clean heart, O God; and renew a right spirit within me.*" Ps. 51:10

1. What goes before? Preceding the experience.
2. What takes place? Possessing the experience.
3. What happens after? Perpetuating the experience.
4. What are the results? The purpose of the experience.
5. What are the dangers? The perils of the experience.

—D. W. Lambert

300. THE BURDEN-BEARING LORD

"*Cast thy burden upon the Lord, and he shall sustain thee.*" Ps. 55:22

Unburdened lives are very few. What burdens does the Lord engage to bear for us?

1. The burden of sin
2. The burden of grief
3. The burden of the future

—Hugh Ross Mackintosh, *Sermons*

301. THE BURDEN BEARER

"*Cast thy burden upon the Lord, and he shall sustain thee.*" Ps. 55:22

Consider:

1. What the burden is.
   a) The burden of remorse
   b) The burden of care
   c) The burden of service
   d) The burden of grief
   e) The burden of fear
   f) The burden of temptation

2. What is to be done with this burden.
   "Cast thy burden on the Lord."
3. What will then happen.
   "He shall sustain thee."

—Unknown

302. THE FLAG

"Thou hast given a banner to them that fear thee, that it may be displayed because of the truth." Ps. 60:4

In Ballarat, Victoria, Australia, I came across some lines—written, I believe, by a local poet—which have haunted me ever since. Here they are:

> Faith is a flag we'll dare to fly,
> Raging wind or frowning sky,
> Mist of fear or starless night:
> Wave the banner, brave and bright.

What are the functions of a banner?

1. It is a signal for war.
2. It is a sign of self-commitment.
3. It is a rallying point for those of common loyalty.

303. IN GOOD TIME

"Early will I seek thee." Ps. 63:1
These words may perhaps be interpreted in three ways.

1. Early in my life will I seek thee.
2. Early in the day will I seek thee.
3. Early in my enterprises will I seek thee.

304. HARVEST LESSONS

"The pastures are clothed with flocks; the valleys also are covered over with corn; they shout for joy, they also sing." Ps. 65:13

Israel looks at its best in the time of harvest. The Psalmist was impressed by the lovely sight of the valleys full of corn. The sight also gladdens our eyes.

What lessons may be learned from it?

1. The lesson of gratitude
2. The lesson of mutual dependence
3. The lesson from natural law

—Henry James Garland

305. NOSTALGIA

"God who brings the lonely home."

Ps. 68:6 Moffatt

1. Nostalgia implies that there is a home.
2. Nostalgia implies that we are away from it.
3. Nostalgia implies that we passionately long to return to it.

306. THE REVELATION OF THE RAIN

"He shall come down like rain upon the mown grass: as showers that water the earth." Ps. 72:6

How does the rain come?

1. Freely
2. Gently
3. Impartially
4. Revivingly

—Walter A. Mursell

307. THE RAIN OF REVIVAL

"He shall come down like rain upon the mown grass." Ps. 72:6

They tell in New Zealand of a little boy living in that country, the son of a famous vocalist, who went with his mother one summer evening to hear his father sing in Mendelssohn's *Elijah*. The auditorium was packed to capacity and the tense appreciative crowd inspired the singer to do his best. Particularly powerful and impressive was his rendering of the aria in which a passionate plea is made for rain. The little fellow listened spellbound as his father poured his soul into the song. When, however, the performance was over and they emerged into the street, the boy was mystified. Rain was coming down in torrents. Recalling that it had been fine when they had gone

131

into the hall, he had his doubts as to the cause of the sudden change in the weather. "Mummy," he asked, "did God think Daddy really meant it?"

When we pray for the rain of revival does God know that we really mean it?

Note four characteristics of such a revival.

1. Like rain, it is heavenly in its source.
2. Like rain, it is free in its bestowal.
3. Like rain, it is impartial in its benefits.
4. Like rain, it is fructifying in its results.

308. THE RIDDLE OF LIFE

"*I was envious at the foolish when I saw the prosperity of the wicked.*"   Ps. 73:3

This man, in telling his own experience, speaks for many. The thinkers of every age have been perplexed by the riddle of life.

1. The riddle unread
2. The riddle misread
3. The riddle reread

—David Burns, *The Song of the Well*

309. WHAT SET HIM RIGHT

"*When I thought to know this, it was too painful for me; until I went into the sanctuary of God.*"
Ps. 73:16-17

He was all wrong, the writer of this psalm, jarred, beaten down, utterly perplexed: all wrong, and he tells us what put him right.

He went into the sanctuary. What did he find there that served to rectify his condition?

1. He found release.
2. He found relationships.
3. He found resources.

—Unknown

310. RECKONING ON GOD

"*But God.*"   Ps. 73:26

Everything the writer believed in had "gone

west." There seemed nothing to live for. Then he began to realize that he was leaving God out of account. "But God!" The words declare the intervention of God in the affairs of men.

1. They ring the alarm of conscience.
2. They sound the death knell of evil.
3. They relight the lamp of hope.
4. They proclaim the certainty of the divine presence.

—Harold T. Barrow

311. THE DARKNESS OF DOUBT

"Hath God forgotten to be gracious? hath he in anger shut up his tender mercies? Selah. And I said, This is my infirmity: but I will remember the years of the right hand of the most High."
Ps. 77:9-10

If your spiritual skies are always blue and your vision of God always clear, this sermon isn't for you. But if it is sometimes otherwise with you—then, read on.

Next time this mood is on us, let us reflect:

1. That we are part of a very goodly company. Elijah in the Old Testament and Paul in the New had just such experiences.
2. That we have struck a bad patch. It will not always be like this.
3. That God once gave us glorious certainty. "I will remember the years of the right hand of the most High."

—J. Ithel Jones, *Expository Times*

312. GOD'S WAY IN THE SANCTUARY

"Thy way, O God, is in the sanctuary."
Ps. 77:13

1. This means that God's way is a way into the sanctuary
   —the way of repentance and faith.
2. This means that God's way is a way within the sanctuary

—the way of worship, study and fellowship.
3. This means that God's way is a way out of
the sanctuary
—the way of witness and service.

313. LIMITING GOD

"Yea, they turned back and tempted God, and
limited the Holy One of Israel." Ps. 78:41

How did these people limit God?

1. By their forgetfulness
"And forgat his works, and his wonders."
(vs. 11)
2. By their lawlessness
"They kept not the covenant of God, and
refused to walk in his law." (vs. 10)
3. By their faithlessness
"Because they believed not in God, and
trusted not in his salvation." (vs. 22)

—Arthur T. Pierson,
The Making of a Sermon

314. LIMITING GOD

"They . . . limited the Holy One of Israel."
Ps. 78:41

1. We limit God in our creed.
2. We limit God in our characters.
3. We limit God in our conduct.
4. We limit God in our careers.

315. LONGING FOR GOD

"My heart and my flesh crieth out for the living
God." Ps. 84:2

There is a difference between crying *to* God and
crying *for* God. The psalmist yearned for the
Lord as blind men long for light. We, too, know
this heart hunger for the divine. What gives rise
to it?

1. The sense of meaninglessness
2. The sense of incompleteness

3. The sense of loneliness
4. The sense of sinfulness

316. SPARROWS AND SWALLOWS

"Yea, the sparrow hath found an house, and the swallow a nest for herself, where she may lay her young, even thine altars, O Lord of hosts, my King, and my God." Ps. 84:3

There is a very shy little thought sheltering like a violet in this lovely verse. It is a thought you may easily miss; and yet a thought which, once found, has a strange way of searching the heart. Why does the psalmist speak of the dwelling of the sparrow as a house and of that of the swallow as a nest? Is it not because the latter is a migrant while the former is not?

Note that the psalmist refers to the "altars" of God. Let us look at three of them.
  1. The altar of dedication
      Are we "sparrows" or "swallows" there?
  2. The altar of supplication
      Are we "sparrows" or "swallows" there?
  3. The altar of adoration
      Are we "sparrows" or "swallows" there?

317. THE "SELAHS" OF LIFE

"Selah." Ps. 84:4

This word "selah" is transliterated rather than translated in our versions because scholars cannot quite make up their minds as to its precise meaning.

Most agree that it was some sort of musical direction, but what exactly they are not sure.

There are several possibilities.
  1. Some say that it called for a changing of the key.
  2. Some say that it signified a pause or rest in the music.

3. Some say it indicated a musical climax and was the signal for a burst of praise.

318. NERVED BY GOD

"*Happy are they who, nerved by thee, set out on pilgrimage!*" Ps. 84:5 Moffatt

There are many things on the pilgrimage which would unnerve us:

1. The almost overpowering sense of loneliness.
2. The distressing doubts which persistently arise and cast long dark shadows on our pathway.
3. The apparent meaninglessness and mystery of things.

—Alwyn Lake Thomas, *Things That Matter*

319. THE LORD GOD AS A SUN

"*The Lord God is a sun and a shield.*"
Ps. 84:11

1. The Lord God is a sun—then my life may illumined.
2. The Lord God is a sun—then my life may be cheered.
3. The Lord God is a sun—then my life may be enriched.
4. The Lord God is a sun—then my life may be rightly centralized.
5. The Lord God is a sun—then my life may be beautiful.

—Joseph Pearce, *The Alabaster Box*

320. GOD AS A SUN

"*The Lord God is a sun.*" Ps. 84:11

1. As a sun God is the source of light.
2. As a sun God is the fount of life.
3. As a sun God is the controlling center of life.
4. As a sun God supports, succors, and sustains life.

321. THE DIVIDED HEART

"*Unite my heart to fear thy name.*"   Ps. 86:11

1. A divided heart means an unhappy heart.
2. A divided heart means an ineffective life.
3. A divided heart is unworthy of God.
   Note: It is only in the fear of God you can really unite the heart. The gracious power of our Lord can unite the most divided heart.

—J. D. Jones,
The Gospel of the Sovereignty

322. GOD'S FAITHFULNESS

"*Nor suffer my faithfulness to fail.*"   Ps. 89:33

1. The contents of God's faithfulness.
2. The constancy of God's faithfulness.
3. The comfort of God's faithfulness.

—Robert Cowan

323. THE JOY OF BEGINNING AGAIN
A NEW YEAR SERMON OUTLINE

"*Thou . . . sayest, Return, ye children of men.*"
Ps. 90:3

1. These words might be written on the flyleaf of the Book of Nature.
2. These words sum up the course of history.
3. These words constitute the challenge of the New Year.
4. These words epitomize the message of Christ.

—C. M. Chavasse

324. THE TELLING OF LIFE'S TALE

"*We spend our years as a tale that is told.*"
Ps. 90:9

1. Like a tale, life is soon told.
2. Like a tale, life is varied.
3. Like a tale, life makes a mark on the minds of those who observe it.

4. Like a tale, life must soon close.

—A. Benfield

325. A TALE THAT IS TOLD

"We spend our years as a tale that is told."

Ps. 90:9

"Every man's life," declared Hans Andersen, "is a fairy tale written by God's fingers."

1. A tale is told by someone.
2. A tale is told about someone.
3. A tale is told to someone.

326. THE STORY OF LIFE

"We spend our years as a tale that is told"

Ps. 90:9

Man has ever been a story teller. One writer, who has delved into the folklore of the ancients, has said concerning the first endeavors of the human mind to understand the mystery of experience: "Life was told in a tale, not explained by a philosophy."

1. A story often has variety.
2. Despite these variations, it can still have one author and one purpose.
3. A story finishes and yet it does not finish.

—R. Brown

327. THE PASSING DAYS

"So teach us to number our days, that we may apply our hearts unto wisdom." Ps. 90:12

The passing of the old year is an occasion for mixed emotions for all serious-minded people. Some make it a time of noisy jollification, but the mood of the psalmist is better suited to the passing year.

Note the unit of measurement—"our days." Why should we so measure our time?

1. Because by so doing we are conforming to a divine arrangement.

The day is God's primary division of time.

2. Because life itself is but a lengthened day. Bishop Hall wrote: "Every day is a little life, and our whole life is but a day repeated."

3. Because by so doing we may apply our hearts the better unto wisdom.

—*Scottish Free Church Record*

328. NUMBERING THE DAYS

"*So teach us to number our days, that we may apply our hearts unto wisdom.*" Ps. 90:12

Who of us has kept a record of the number of days he has lived to date? We know how many years we have lived; but, for most of us, it would call for considerable calculation to ascertain the exact total of our days.

Why do we need to take special note of the days?

1. Because days are the primary divine standard of measurement.

Man has fixed the calendar year, but God has determined the length of each day.

2. Because days are more readily reckoned than years.

3. Because days may be all that remain to us. There may be no years to calculate.

329. HOW DO WE MEASURE LIFE?

"*So teach us to number our days, that we may apply our hearts unto wisdom.*" Ps. 90:12

1. Shall we measure it from the standpoint of years?

2. Shall we measure it in terms of wealth?

3. Shall we not rather measure it by character?

—Alwyn Lake Thomas, *Things that Matter*

330. THE SHADOW OF THE ALMIGHTY

"*He that dwelleth in the secret place of the most High shall abide under the shadow of the Almighty.*" Ps. 91:1

1. A shadow cannot exist apart from some substance.
2. A shadow cannot continue save in proximity to the substance.
3. Shadows are deepest on brightest days.
4. Some day there will be no shadow.

331. THE PERILS OF PROSPERITY

"*The destruction that wasteth at noonday.*"

Ps. 91:6

Of all the bombs that fell on London during the war the worst were those dropped in broad daylight. I used regularly to visit a woman in a mental hospital who was shopping at noon one summer day in a busy, eastern suburb of the city, when a guided missile exploded in the midst of the crowd. Though herself unharmed, the sight bereft the poor woman permanently of her reason.

So with the moral perils of the noonday. They are perhaps the most deadly of all.

1. Think of the perils of prosperity in the life of a nation.
2. Think of the perils of prosperity in the life of the Church.
3. Think of the perils of prosperity in the life of the individual.

332. RELIGION AND LONGEVITY

"*With long life will I satisfy him.*" Ps. 91:16

True religion promotes longevity:

1. Because it teaches the proper care of the body.
2. Because it protects against all that would destroy health.
3. Because it removes worry.

4. Because it proclaims the fact of immortality.

—T. De Witt Talmage

333. THE HIGHEST HELP ONLY CAN SATISFY OUR NEEDS

"It is a good thing to give thanks unto the Lord, and to sing praises unto thy name, O most High."

Ps. 92:1

Only the highest can really help us:
1. In temptation
2. In sorrow
3. In doubt
4. In sin

—Phillips Brooks

334. THE STRENGTH OF THE HILLS

"The strength of the hills is his also."

Ps. 95:4

In what does the strength of the hills consist?
1. Beauty
2. Permanence
3. Atmosphere
4. Outlook

—Walter A. Mursell

335. HE OWNS THE SEA

"The sea is his, and he made it."

Ps. 95:5

1. The beauty of the sea
2. The power of the sea
3. The abundance of the sea
4. The purification of the sea

336. THE SOVEREIGNTY OF GOD

"The Lord reigneth: let the earth rejoice."

Ps. 97:1

"The Lord reigneth; let the people tremble."

Ps. 99:1

I have chosen my two texts just because they set

forth a double result that will follow upon a realization of the truth of the sovereignty of God.

1. We shall gain a new sense of awe.
   "The Lord reigneth; let the people tremble."
2. We shall acquire a new confidence in the coming of a better day.
   "The Lord reigneth; let the earth rejoice."
3. We shall have calm and peace amid the varied experiences of our individual lives.

—J. D. Jones,
The Gospel of the Sovereignty

337. SIN AND SALVATION

Ps. 103:1-5

Here we find:

1. The three facts of sin
   a) Its guilt
      "Who forgiveth all thine iniquities."
   b) Its stain
      "Who healeth all thy diseases."
   c) Its power
      "Who redeemeth thy life from destruction."
2. The three facts of salvation
   a) He forgiveth.
   b) He healeth.
   c) He redeemeth.

—Henry Drummond

338. HOMILETIC HEXAPLA

"Bless the Lord, O my soul: and all that is within me, bless his holy name. . . . Who forgiveth all thine iniquities; who healeth all thy diseases; who redeemeth thy life from destruction; who crowneth thee with loving kindness and tender mercies; who satisfieth thy mouth with good things; so that thy youth is renewed like the eagle's." Ps. 103:1-5

1. Three blights removed
   a) Guilt put away
   b) Corruption banished

c) Destruction averted
2. Three blessings bestowed
   a) Favors that gratify
   b) Pleasures that can satisfy
   c) Life that can never die
                              —W. Durban

339. FIVE VIVID SCENES

"Bless the Lord, O my soul, and forget not all his benefits." Ps. 103:2

1. A scene in a court of law
   "Who forgiveth all thine iniquities."
                              (vs. 3a)
2. A scene in a hospital ward
   "Who healeth all thy diseases." (vs. 3b)
3. A scene in a slave market
   "Who redeemeth thy life from destruction." (vs. 4a)
4. A scene in a throne room
   "Who crowneth thee with lovingkindness and tender mercies." (vs. 4b)
5. A scene in a banqueting hall
   "Who satisfieth thy mouth with good things; so that thy youth is renewed like the eagle's." (vs. 5)
                              —Alexander Whyte

340. WHAT TO DO AT THE NEW YEAR

"Bless the Lord, O my soul, and forget not all his benefits." Ps. 103:2

1. Remember
2. Rejoice
3. Reflect
4. Resolve
                              —David Hogg

341. THERE GO THE SHIPS

"There go the ships." Ps. 104:26

1. There goes a ship—the ship that took Paul to Philippi in Greece.

2. There goes a ship—the ship that brought Augustine to England.

3. There goes a ship—the ship that carried Columbus to America.

4. There goes a ship—the ship that transported the Pilgrims to the new world.

5. There goes a ship—the ship that conveyed William Carey to India.

—Newell Dwight Hillis, *The American Pulpit*

342. A CHRISTMAS MEDITATION

"*My meditation of Him shall be sweet: I will be glad in the Lord.*" Ps. 104:34

It is always sweet to meditate upon the Lord, but particularly so at the Christmas season. Here are three sublime matters on this subject upon which to meditate:

1. Jesus had a heavenly father and an earthly mother.

2. Jesus left a heavenly throne for an earthly stable.

3. Jesus came to establish a heavenly kingdom in an earthly setting.

—W. M. Tanner

343. ON BEING A PRAYER

"*But I———prayer.*" Ps. 109:4

Here is a man who is not merely deciding to pray, but to be a prayer. You will notice that the words "give myself unto" in your Bible are printed in italics. This means that they do not appear in the original, but have been added by the translators to fill out the sense. Unhappily, they have the unintended effect of detracting somewhat from the vigor of the utterance.

"I———prayer." What does that involve? The answer is wrapped up with the nature of prayer itself. How, then, are we to define prayer? I offer three replies:

1. Prayer is giving as well as receiving.

2. Prayer is listening as well as speaking.

3. Prayer is co-operating as well as submitting.

344. SINNING IN PRAYER

"When he shall be judged, let him be condemned: and let his prayer become sin." Ps. 109:7

Is it possible that we can actually sin while engaging in prayer? Yes, it is. Think this through.

1. We sin in prayer if we rush into God's presence without realizing to whom we are coming.

2. We sin in prayer if we fail to come before him in deep humility, confessing our unworthiness and acknowledging our nothingness.

3. We sin in prayer when we approach the throne of grace with unconfessed sin in our lives.

4. We sin in prayer when we are presumptuous in our asking.

5. We sin in prayer when our motive in asking is anything less than the glory of God.

345. THE BROOK BY THE WAY

"He shall drink of the brook in the way: therefore shall he lift up the head." Ps. 110:7

1. The brook of delight by the way of duty

2. The brook of devotion by the way of doctrine

3. The brook of development by the way of demand

Result: "Therefore shall he lift up the head."

346. THE NEW HEART

"His heart is established." Ps. 112:8

"Enlarge my heart." Ps. 119:32

"My heart is inditing [literally, 'bubbling up with'] a good matter." Ps. 45:1

Christianity is a religion of newness. It begins

145

with a new birth and it ends with a new earth; it starts with a new creature and it finishes with a new creation; it opens with a new kind of man and it closes with a new mankind.

Central among all the new things introduced by it is the new heart. What are that heart's salient features?

1. It is established.
2. It is enlarged.
3. It is effervescent.

347. A CALL TO THANKSGIVING

"Praise ye the Lord. Praise, O ye servants of the Lord, praise the name of the Lord." Ps. 113:1

How strongly the note of thanksgiving to God is sounded in the Bible! Is that note sufficiently prominent in our lives? Our text is a call to it. "Praise ye the Lord. Praise, O ye servants of the Lord, praise the name of the Lord."

1. Who are to praise the Lord?
   "His servants."
2. What are they to praise?
   "The name of the Lord."
3. When are they to praise?
   "From the rising of the sun unto the going down of the same." (vs. 3)
4. How are they to praise the Lord?
   "Praise him with the sound of the trumpet: praise him with the psaltery and harp."
   Ps. 150:3

—J. Allan Wright

348. VOWS

"I will pay my vows unto the Lord now in the presence of all his people." Ps. 116:14

1. Vows should be made at the right time.
2. Vows should be made in the right company.
3. Vows must be paid to the right person.

—Herbert H. Farmer, *The Healing Cross*

349. THE BIBLE IN A BOY'S HEART

"Thy word have I hid in mine heart, that I might not sin against thee." PSALM 119:11

1. The best Book
   "Thy word"
2. The best place
   "Mine heart"
3. The best purpose
   "That I might not sin against thee"

—Andrew W. Blackwood,
Planning a Year's Pulpit Work

350. WHERE TO HAVE THE BIBLE

"Thy word have I hid in mine heart, that I might not sin against thee." Ps. 119:11

1. It is good to have the Book in the hand.
2. It is better to have the Book in the head.
3. It is best to have the Book in the heart.

—Andrew W. Blackwood,
Planning a Year's Pulpit Work

351. THE FIVE LAWS

"Give me understanding, and I shall keep thy law; yea, I shall observe it with my whole heart."
Ps. 119:34

There are five main laws in accordance with which men may regulate their lives:

1. The law of the land
2. The law of custom and social usage
3. The law of current public opinion
4. The law of conscience
5. The law of God

352. THE PROCESSIONAL OF LIFE

"Thy statutes have been my songs in the house of my pilgrimage." Ps. 119:54

The New Year will be good throughout if we step to this music.

By what process does law become thus lyrical?

147

1. Through clearer knowledge
2. Through warmer love
3. Through persistent obedience

—W. L. Watkinson,
The Education of the Heart

353. FORTUNATE MISFORTUNE

"*It is good for me to have been in trouble.*"
Ps. 119:71 Moffatt

1. Misfortune serves to deepen life.
2. Misfortune is often the means of releasing undreamed of powers.
3. Misfortune brings enlarged capacity to understand and help other people.
4. Misfortune can make real and vital one's relationship to God.

—William M. Elliott

354. THE SETTLED WORD OF GOD

"*For ever, O Lord, thy word is settled in heaven.*"
Ps. 119:89

1. Where it is settled.
   "In heaven"
2. Why it is settled.
   Because it is the word of God.
3. For how long it is settled.
   "For ever"

—Unknown

355. HALF-HEARTED

"*I hate men who are half and half.*"
Ps. 119:113 Moffatt

1. Some men never put their heart into anything.
2. Some men are halfhearted.
3. Some men are wholehearted.

356. HALF AND HALF

"*I hate men who are half and half.*"
Ps. 119:113 Moffatt

Like the psalmist:

1. We hate men who are half and half because we never know which half of them represents their real self.

   A friend of mine approaching a large house in London was challenged by a huge dog. It was barking savagely at one end of its body and wagging its tail at the other. My friend halted, uncertain of its intentions. "I didn't know which end to believe," he said. So here.

2. We hate those who are half and half because by their attitude they betray the fact that they do not sufficiently realize the urgency of the issues of life.

3. We hate those who are half and half because, being incapable of enthusiasm themselves, they kindle none in us.

357. VERIFYING THE WORD

"The sum of thy commands is truth."
Ps. 119:160 Moffatt

1. We verify the Bible by looking back.
   Archaeology is constantly confirming the testimony of the sacred volume.
2. We verify the Bible by looking around.
   All that is best in contemporary civilization can be traced back, in one way or another, to the Word of God.
3. We verify the Bible by looking within.
   The work of God in our own hearts and lives is strong corroboration of its veracity.
4. We verify the Bible by looking above.
   In prayer we actually encounter the eternal Being of whom we read in the pages of Holy Writ.

358. THE CALL OF THE HILLS

"I will lift up mine eyes unto the hills."
Ps. 121:1

The speaker, as we take it, was one of the

Jews in Babylon. The great plain, arched by the round sky, was his temple; but, as he closed his eyes to pray, he saw the blue hills of Judah and the towers that crowned the house of the Lord.

"I will lift up mine eyes," he cried, "unto the hills."

So may we.

1. I will lift up mine eyes unto the hills and let my spirit speed home.
2. I will lift up mine eyes unto the hills and let my spirit take rest.
3. I will lift up mine eyes unto the hills and let my spirit gain health.

—David Burns, *The Song of the Well*

359. THE DIVINE DOUBTLESS

"He that goeth forth and weepeth, bearing precious seed, shall doubtless come again with rejoicing, bringing his sheaves with him." Ps. 126:6

1. This is the doubtless of invariable law.
2. This is the doubtless of divine providence.
3. This is the doubtless of invincible faith.

360. GIFTS TO THE SLEEPING

"He giveth his beloved sleep." Ps. 127:2

As we think of it, we find that in this one precious gift there are really three givings:

1. There is the giving of sleep.
2. There is the giving in sleep.
3. There is the giving by sleep.

—David Burns, *The Song of the Well*

361. CONTRACTING OUT

"Neither do I exercise myself in great matters, or things too high for me." Ps. 131:1

What mental attitude do these words reflect?

1. It might be modesty.
2. It might be indolence.
3. It might be indifference.

362. HARPS AND WILLOWS

"We hanged our harps upon the willows."
Ps. 137:2

1. All God's people have their joy—
   otherwise, why the harp?
2. All God's people have their sorrow—
   otherwise, why hang it up?
3. All God's people have their hope—
   otherwise, why not break the harp in
   pieces?

—Unknown

363. THE DEAD WEIGHT OF ENVIRONMENT

"How shall we sing the Lord's song in a strange land?"   Ps. 137:4

1. How many there are today whose physical surroundings make it hard, if not impossible, to sing the Lord's song!
2. How many there are whose own past makes it hard for them to sing the Lord's song!
3. How many there are who feel that there are special features in the world of our time which make it hard for us to sing the Lord's song!

Adapted.
—W. Mackintosh Mackay,
Problems in Living

364. OUR BESETTING GOD

Ps. 139

1. God in the world within
   (vss. 1-6)
2. God in the world without
   (vss. 7-12)
3. God in the world behind
   (vss. 13-18)
4. God in the world beneath
   (vss. 19-24)

365. THE BESETMENT OF GOD

"Thou hast beset me behind and before, and laid thine hand upon me."   Ps. 139:5

God besets me:
1. Behind.
   All my yesterdays are covered. He saves me from my soiled past.
2. Before.
   All my tomorrows are anticipated. He is undertaking for my future.
3. Just here.
   In this very present, he lays his hand upon me.

—W. E. Sangster,
The Craft of Sermon Construction

366. THE ATMOSPHERE

"Whither shall I flee from thy presence"

Ps. 139:7

1. The atmosphere sustains.
2. The atmosphere presses.
   Fifteen pounds to the square inch. "A man can as soon pass out of the atmosphere in which he breathes," wrote Alexander Maclaren, "as he can pass out of the love of God."
3. The atmosphere protects.
   Think of a meteor flashing across the sky, disintegrating in a blaze of glory as it enters the gaseous envelope in which the earth is enclosed.
4. The atmosphere transmits.
5. The atmosphere tempers.
   "We owe the sun to the atmosphere which tempers its brightness," declared Joseph Parker, "and we cannot amend God's way of coming to us."
6. The atmosphere reflects.
7. The atmosphere reveals.
8. The atmosphere revives.

—F. E. Marsh, *Emblems of the Holy Spirit*

367. THE SIGH OF THE SINCERE

"Search me, O God, and know my heart: try me, and know my thoughts: And see if there be any wicked way in me, and lead me in the way everlasting." Ps. 139:23-24

Observe here:

1. The examination invoked.
   a) Its range
      "Search me, O God."
   b) Its depth
      "And know my thoughts."
   c) Its severity
      "Try me."
2. The design of this examination.
   a) Deliverance from our own way of life
   b) Guidance in God's way

—W. L. Watkinson, *The Fatal Barter*

368. MEMORY

"They shall abundantly utter the memory of thy great goodness." Ps. 145:7

Some people have very retentive memories. Cyrus, for example, is said to have known by name every soldier in his army. And the martyrs, Cranmer and Ridley, learned the whole of the New Testament by heart.

1. Memory is the faculty by which we retain and recall our knowledge of the past, the gift which conserves the collection made by sensation, perception, and attention.
2. Our retrospect gives us cause for contrition.
3. With regard to some of us, hope's basket, as far as this world is concerned, is nearly empty, while memory's sack is full.

—*Scottish Free Church Record*

369. GOD'S WAY OF PROVIDING

"Thou openest thine hand, and satisfiest the desire of every living thing." Ps. 145:16

How does God provide?

153

1. He provides personally.
   "Thou."
2. He provides easily.
   "Openest thine hand."
3. He provides abundantly.
   "And satisfiest the desire of every living thing."

—Quoted by T. Harwood Pattison,
The Making of the Sermon

370. GOD—THE REBUILDER

"The Lord doth build up Jerusalem: he gathereth together the outcasts of Israel. He healeth the broken in heart, and bindeth up their wounds. He telleth the number of the stars; he calleth them all by their names." Ps. 147:2-4

Here we see:

1. God rebuilding a place for himself.
   "The Lord doth build up Jerusalem."
2. God rebuilding a place for humanity.
   "He gathereth together the outcasts."
3. God rebuilding human character.
   "He healeth the broken in heart, and bindeth up their wounds."
4. God rebuilding the world of nature.
   "He telleth the number of the stars; he calleth them all by their names."

—E. T. Evans, *The Vision of Victory*

371. MERCIES ON THE MOUNTAINS

"[He] maketh grass to grow upon the mountains."
Ps. 147:8

1. God's treasures are often found in the most unexpected places.
2. God's provision is sure in the most adverse circumstances.
3. God's signposts to blessing are often man's obstacles.
4. God's rewards are found by those who climb the mountains.

—John L. Bird

372. THE WIND

"He causeth his wind to blow." Ps. 147:18

1. Wind is invisible in its essence.
2. Wind is unconfined in its operations.
3. Wind is mysterious in its action.
4. Wind is powerful in its movements.
5. Wind is cleansing in its sweep.
6. Wind is withering in its work.
7. Wind is varied in its direction.

—F. E. Marsh, *Emblems of the Holy Spirit*

PROVERBS

373. THE PATH OF THE JUST

"The path of the just . . . shineth more and more unto the perfect day." Prov. 4:18

1. It is a plain path.
2. It is a bright path.
3. It is a sure path.

—Unknown

374. THE PATH OF THE PERFECT

"The path of the just is as the shining light, that shineth more and more unto the perfect day."
Prov. 4:18

1. It is an upward path.
2. It is a winding path.
3. It is a shining path.

—Unknown

375. ANGLING FOR SOULS

"He that [angleth] for souls is wise."
Prov. 11:30

Four effective points on this topic may be made of Izaac Walton's famous advice to fishermen:

155

1. Be sure your face is toward the light.
2. Study the fish's curious ways.
3. Then keep yourself well out of sight.
4. And cherish patience all your days.

376. BUYING THE TRUTH

"Buy the truth, and sell it not."

PROV. 23:23

1. The greatness of truth
   "Buy . . . sell not."
2. Buy the truth:
   a) No matter what it cost
   b) In preference to everything else
   c) Even if you have to part with everything to secure it
   d) As much of it as you can
   e) In every shape and form
   f) To be a possession of your own
3. Sell it not:
   a) Whatever may be offered to you instead of it.
   b) You will never be called upon to sell it.
   c) You will always have need of it.
   d) You will never find anything that can take its place.

—David Roberts

377. GIVE ME THINE HEART

"My son, give me thine heart." PROV. 23:26

1. The relationship
   "My son"
2. The request
   "Give me"
3. The requirement
   "Thine heart"

—Mary G. Brainard

378. GOOD NEWS FOR A BAD WORLD

"As cold waters to a thirsty soul, so is good news from a far country." PROV. 25:25

The gospel is good news for people:

1. Up in the North
2. Over in the East
3. Out in the West
4. Down in the South

—Andrew W. Blackwood,
Planning a Year's Pulpit Work

379. THE UNKNOWN FUTURE

"Thou knowest not what a day may bring forth."
PROV. 27:1

Consider:

1. The fact that we are ignorant of the future.
2. The pity that we are ignorant of the future.
3. The mercy that we are ignorant of the future.

I know not what awaits me,
God *kindly* veils my eyes.

380. THE VALUE OF VISION

"Where there is no vision, the people cast off restraint: but he that keepeth the law, happy is he." PROV. 29:18 R.S.V.

1. Visions explain
    The key to the riddle of the seen is to be found in the unseen.
2. Visions restrain
    "Where there is no vision, the people cast off restraint."
3. Visions sustain
    "Where there is no vision, the people perish." (K.J.V.)

381. WEE BUT WISE

(A Children's Address Outline)
"There be four things which are little upon the earth, but they are exceeding wise: The ants are a people not strong, yet they prepare their meat in the summer; The conies are but a feeble folk, yet make they their houses in the rocks; The locusts have no king, yet go they forth all of

157

them by bands; The spider taketh hold with
her hands, and is in kings' palaces."

PROV. 30:24-28

How may you be wise though wee? By being:

1. Busy like the ant.
    Cf. French fable of ant and grasshopper.
2. Building like the cony.
    Conies are not strong in themselves but
    strong in their position.
3. Banded like the locust.
    A single locust is but a puny insect; a
    swarm of locusts is a formidable army.
4. Billeted like the spider.
    Who lives in Buckingham Palace? The
    Queen? Yes. But I am sure that some-
    where there also lives—a spider.

382. THE SPIDER IN PALACES

"The spider taketh hold with her hands, and is in
kings' palaces." PROV. 30:28

There are several lessons which the text teaches:

1. Divine mechanism is quite exquisite.
2. Insignificance is no excuse for inaction.
3. Repulsiveness and loathsomeness will some-
    times climb into very elevated places.
4. Perseverance will mount into a king's
    palace.

—T. De Witt Talmage

ECCLESIASTES

383. THE PROFIT OF TOIL

"What profit hath he that worketh in that wherein
he laboureth?" ECCL. 3:9

To this cynical question we may return three replies. There is:

1. The profit of personal enhancement.

2. The profit of practical achievement.
3. The profit of social advancement.

384. ETERNITY IN THE HEART

"He hath set eternity in their heart."
ECCL. 3:11 R.V. Margin

God has set eternity in our hearts:

1. As a microphone, through which he may broadcast to our whole personality his mind and will.
2. As a microcosm, a miniature representation of the eternal world of God's truth which is our real home.
3. As a microscope, by which we can test and analyze all life and know which are the things most worthwhile.

—John H. Withers, *Speak for Yourself*

385. MISTAKEN SIGNS

"Say not thou, What is the cause that the former days were better than these? for thou dost not enquire wisely concerning this." ECCL. 7:10

Some say:

1. "I am not so happy as I once was."
2. "I am not so holy as I once was."
3. "I do not love God as I once did."
4. "I do not make the rapid progress I once did."

—W. L. Watkinson, *Mistaken Signs*

386. THE POOR WISE MAN

"There was a little city, and few men within it; and there came a great king against it, and besieged it, and built great bulwarks against it: Now there was found in it a poor wise man, and he by his wisdom delivered the city; yet no man remembered that same poor man." ECCL. 9:14-15

1. What is the city?
   It is the world.
2. Who is the great king?
   It is Satan.

3. Who is the poor wise man?
   It is Christ.
      Note:
         a) What he does
            "Delivered the city."
         b) How he does it
            "By his wisdom."
         c) What happens
            "No man remembered."
                              —M. B. Tanner

387. THE INFLUENCE OF ONE BAD MAN

"One sinner destroyeth much good."

ECCL. 9:18

The influence of a bad man may be considered:
   1. Negatively
      The good prevented
   2. Positively
      The evil done
   3. Consciously
      What is wrought deliberately
   4. Unconsciously
      What is wrought unwittingly
   5. Immediately
      The direct result of sin
   6. Remotely
      The long-term issue

—Arthur T. Pierson,
The Making of a Sermon

388. NOTHING VENTURE, NOTHING WIN

"He that observeth the wind shall not sow; and
he that regardeth the clouds shall not reap."

ECCL. 11:4

   1. A restraint that can go too far
      The man who is over cautious will miss
      life's opportunities. He must not let the
      difficulties blind him to the opportunities.
   2. A risk that must be taken
   3. A reaping that will ultimately ensue
      The man who does not fear the risk of

faith will reap the reward of faith.

—R. G. Crawford

389. THE LAND OF BIG THINGS

"Rejoice, O young man, in thy youth."

Eccl. 11:9

Youth demands a large territory. It boldly pegs out an extensive claim. "Rejoice, O young man, in thy youth." Why rejoice? Just because it is an estate so vast, a land of such big things and of such boundless possibilities.

What, then, are some of the big things to be found in the land of youth?

1. There is its big expectation of life.
2. There are its big ideas.
3. There are its big opportunities.
4. There are its big decisions.

—W. G. Branch, *In the Days of Thy Youth*

390. REMEMBERING THE CREATOR

"Remember now thy Creator in the days of thy youth." Eccl. 12:1

1. Remember thy Creator in youth because youth has a good memory.
2. Remember thy Creator in youth because youth is in peculiar peril of forgetting.
3. Remember thy Creator in youth because by so doing you will affect your whole life for good.
4. Remember thy Creator in youth because he remembered you in his youth.

   Not one golden hair was grey
   Upon his crucifixion day.

SONG OF SOLOMON

391. THE LITTLE FOXES

"Take us the foxes, the little foxes, that spoil the vines: for our vines have tender grapes."

Song of S. 2:15

What are the little foxes that spoil the spiritual life?

1. Little sins
2. Little negligences
3. Little ignorances

—Elmitt Browne

392. A WALLED GARDEN

"A garden inclosed." Song of S. 4:12

Tucked away in that strange and little-read book, the Song of Solomon, is a most suggestive phrase, descriptive of the Christian life. "A garden inclosed."

"Inclosed." The word suggests:

1. The privacy from observation which love can enjoy in such a garden.
   Here we have:
   a) A truth concerning the inwardness of Christian experience.
   b) A test concerning the quality of Christian experience.
2. The variety of occupation that love can find in such a garden.
   Think:
   a) How differently Christ will come to us.
   b) How continually Christ will abide in us.
3. The hospitality to others that love can dispense in such a garden.
   Consider:
   a) The produce of the garden that can be shared.
   b) The praise of the Gardener that will be given.

—G. B. Duncan,
Wanting the Impossible

393. THE DOVE

"My dove, my undefiled." Song of S. 6:9

Spiritualize this ancient Hebrew love poem and

you have here the language of our Lord to his church. "My dove." What does that suggest and signify?

1. The dove is clean in its nature.
2. The dove is gentle in its manner.
3. The dove is constant in its love.
4. The dove is swift in its flight.
5. The dove is beautiful in its plumage.
6. The dove is social in its habits.

—F. E. Marsh, *Emblems of the Holy Spirit*

ISAIAH

394. THE HIGHEST EDUCATION

"*Learn to do well.*" Isa. 1:17

We hear much of primary, secondary, and higher education, but the text reminds us of a sphere yet beyond these levels. This highest level of education concerns all; securing it is the main end of life.

To acquire this we need:

1. Pattern
2. Power
3. Practice

—W. L. Watkinson,
The Bane and the Antidote

395. THE REASONABLENESS OF GOD

"*Come now, and let us reason together, saith the Lord.*" Isa. 1:18

"God reasons with man. This," says the great expositor, George Adam Smith, "is the first article of religion according to Isaiah." Surely it is a stupendous thing that the divine being should thus condescend to enter into controversy with his puny human creatures!

1. What a compliment to human intelligence!
2. What a revelation of the rationality of life!
3. What a prospect for the happy solution of our human problems!

396. THE PARABLE OF THE VINEYARD

Isa. 5:1-4

1. Its location
   "A very fruitful hill"
2. Its delimitation
   "He fenced it"
3. Its cultivation
   "And gathered out the stones"
4. Its plantation
   "And planted it with the choicest vines"
5. Its fortification
   "And built a tower"
6. Its obligation
   "And he looked that it should bring forth grapes"

397. THE DIVINE DILEMMA

"What could have been done more that I have not done?" Isa. 5:4

What more could God have done:

1. Creatively?
2. Providentially?
3. Redemptively?

398. VISION IN THE TEMPLE

Isa. 6:1-8

1. Isaiah saw the Lord.
   "I saw also the Lord sitting upon a throne." (vs. 1)
2. Isaiah saw himself.
   "Then said I, Woe is me! for I am undone." (vs. 5)
3. Isaiah saw the people.

"I dwell in the midst of a people of unclean lips." (vs. 5)

—W. J. Peacock

399. ISAIAH LOOKED THREE WAYS

Isa. 6:1-9

1. He looked upward.
   "I saw also the Lord, sitting upon a throne." (vs. 1)
2. He looked inward.
   "Woe is me!" (vs. 5)
3. He looked outward.
   "Send me." (vs. 8)

—Desmond Thomas

400. LIFE AT ITS BEST

"Above it stood the seraphims; each one had six wings; with twain he covered his face, and with twain he covered his feet, and with twain he did fly." Isa. 6:2

This is an inspired poet's description of life at its best. It is a prophet's way of describing the ideal life. It is life clothed with wings—wings that are paired in a holy trinity.

What, then, are the marks of life at its best?

1. The first mark of life at its best is the spirit of reverence.
   "With twain he covered his face."
2. The second note in the ideal life is the spirit of humility.
   "With twain he covered his feet." If his face was covered so that he might not see, his feet were covered with his wings so that he might not be seen.
3. The third quality in life at its best is the spirit of service.
   "With twain he did fly."

—Hugh T. Kerr, *The Highway of Life*

401. GUILTY OF SILENCE

"*I am guilty of silence.*" Isa. 6:5
The Englishman's Bible

Are we guilty of silence:

1. In the matter of private prayer?
2. In the matter of our confession of sins and faults?
3. In the matter of evangelism?
4. In the matter of publicly rebuking the wrongs of the world?

402. THE LIVE COAL AND THE LIVING ANSWER

"*Then flew one of the seraphims unto me, having a living coal in his hand, which he had taken with the tongs from off the altar: And he laid it on my mouth, and said, Lo, this hath touched thy lips, and thine iniquity is taken away, and thy sin purged. Also I heard the voice of the Lord, saying, Whom shall I send, and who will go for us? Then said I, Here am I, send me.*"
Isa. 6:6-8

We see here three things:

1. Awareness of sin
2. Assurance of pardon
3. Alacrity in service

403. WHY ANGELS DO NOT PREACH THE GOSPEL

"*Whom shall I send, and who will go for us?*"
Isa. 6:8

What a question for God to ask! Surrounded as he was, in Isaiah's vision, by myriads of angelic messengers, beings capable of speeding on his errands with a velocity surpassing that of light, nevertheless he exclaims, "Whom shall I send?" and is not satisfied until a young man responds. Angels have on occasion proclaimed the gospel, but they are not its normal ministers.

Why?
1. Because such angels do not know the meaning of sin.
2. Because angels do not know the meaning of faith.
3. Because angels do not know the meaning of mortality.

404. THE JOY OF HARVEST

"They joy before thee according to the joy in harvest." Isa. 9:3

What is the joy of harvest? It is:

1. The joy of hope fulfilled.
2. The joy of work completed.
3. The joy of wants supplied.

—John C. Lambert, *The Omnipotent Cross*

405. THE FOURFOLD NAME

"His name shall be called Wonderful, Counsellor, The mighty God, the everlasting Father, The Prince of Peace." Isa. 9:6

1. I am a pilgrim needing a guide—
   He is the Wonderful Counsellor.
2. I am a struggler needing power—
   He is the mighty God.
3. I am a child needing succor—
   He is the everlasting Father.
4. I am a subject needing a king—
   He is the Prince of Peace.

406. THE ZEAL OF THE LORD

"The zeal of the Lord of hosts will perform this."
Isa. 9:7

Our God is not deaf nor dumb nor stony. He does not live in some eternal calm untroubled by the needs and wants of men and the woes and miseries of the world. Amongst the many qualities of his nature is the quality of zeal.

1. Think of the zeal of the Lord in the matter of human redemption.

167

2. Think of the zeal of the Lord in the matter of cleansing and purifying character.
3. Think of the zeal of the Lord for the creation of the new earth.

—J. D. Jones,
The Gospel of the Sovereignty

407. THE LEADERSHIP OF A CHILD

"And a little child shall lead them." Isa. 11:6

1. The days of childhood lead, form, and fix the future history and destiny.
2. The traits of childhood lead the way in all virtues of character.
3. The spirit of childhood leads in influence upon human society.

—Arthur T. Pierson, *The Making of a Sermon*

408. TWILIGHT

"The twilight I longed for
has been turned for me into trembling."

Isa. 21:4 R.S.V.

1. The attraction of the twilight

"The twilight I longed for." Especially in lands where in daytime the sun is strong and the heat oppressive, twilight brings rest and relief, a time for social fellowship and relaxation.

Twilight in another sense may also have its attractions. Many people are content to live in a twilight concerning beliefs and standards of conduct.

2. The dangers of the twilight

"The twilight I longed for
has been turned for me into trembling."

a) We need definite beliefs.
b) We need definite standards of conduct.

3. The transience of the twilight

It does not last long. Either darkness or dawn soon follows. Which is it to be for us? Jesus said, "I am the light of the world: he that followeth me shall not

walk in darkness, but shall have the light
of life" (John 8:12).

—J. Allan Wright

409. WATCHMAN, WHAT OF THE NIGHT?
Isa. 21:11

1. What of the night of sense and sin?
2. What of the night of suffering and sorrow?
3. What of the night of mocking and mystery?
4. What of the night of solitude and separation?

—John Robertson

410. THE PERFECT PEACE OF GOD
"*Thou wilt keep him in perfect peace, whose mind*
is stayed on thee: because he trusteth in thee."
Isa. 26:3

This peace is:

1. Perfect in its quality
   There is an imperfect peace:
   a) the peace of ignorance
   b) the peace of stagnation
   c) the peace of indifference
2. Perfect in its quantity
   The supply is sufficient. The marginal
   rendering of "perfect peace" is "peace,
   peace," that is, "double peace."
3. Perfect in its constancy
   "Thou wilt keep him."

—Unknown

411. MOMENTOUS MOMENTS
"*I will water it every moment.*" Isa. 27:3

"The significance of the moment grows upon
us the more we ponder it. We can never tell
how much we may be affected by any tick of the
clock, so big with fate are the fugitive, elusive
moments." (Watkinson.)

Consider:

1. The moment of temptation

"And the devil took him up, and showed
him all the kingdoms of the world in
a moment of time." Luke 4:5 R.S.V.

2. The moment of tribulation

"Hide thyself . . . for a little moment, until
the indignation be overpast." Isa. 26:20

3. The moment of transformation

"We shall be changed, In a moment, in
the twinkling of an eye."

I Cor. 15:51-52

412. THE GREAT TRUMPET

"And it shall come to pass in that day, that the
great trumpet shall be blown." Isa. 27:13

Listen to six blasts on that trumpet:

1. The blast of alarm
2. The blast of recruitment
3. The blast of assault
4. The blast of retreat
5. The blast of victory
6. The blast of reveille

—T. De Witt Talmage

413. THE CHLOROFORMED SOUL

"It shall be as when an hungry man dreameth,
and, behold, he eateth; but he awaketh, and his
soul is empty: or as when a thirsty man dreameth,
and, behold, he drinketh; but he awaketh, and,
behold, he is faint, and his soul hath appetite:
so shall the multitude of all the nations be, that
fight against mount Zion." Isa. 29:8

1. The pitiful illusion

"It shall be as when a hungry man
dreameth, and, behold, he eateth."

2. The bitter awakening

"But he awaketh, and his soul is empty."

3. The satisfying reality

An Eastern traveler confessed that he had
been so often deceived by the mirage that

when at last he saw the sea he could not believe that it was the sea, he thought it a bigger mirage than usual.

The hungry dreamer can awake to find the bread of life.

—W. L. Watkinson,
The Education of the Heart

414. THE PRIVILEGES OF A MAN OF GOD

"*He shall dwell on high: his place of defence shall be the munitions of rocks: bread shall be given him; his waters shall be sure. Thine eyes shall see the king in his beauty: they shall behold the land that is far off.*" Isa. 33:16-17

Note here:

1. His position
   "He shall dwell on high."
2. His provision
   "Bread shall be given him; his waters shall be sure."
3. His protection
   "His place of defence shall be the munitions of rocks."
4. The promise
   "Thine eyes shall see the king in his beauty."

—Arthur S. Hoyt, *The Work of Preaching*

415. THE LAME TAKING THE PREY

"*The lame take the prey.*" Isa. 33:23

1. Generally, lame people of every sort miss the prey or the prizes of life.
2. It is otherwise in God's plan and in spiritual experience.
3. For blessing we must know our lameness.
   Note: Think of Jacob at Peniel, Mephibosheth at King David's table. God's best gifts are on the lowest shelf.

—F. B. Meyer

171

416. AN ORTHOPAEDIC GOSPEL

"Then shall the lame man leap as an hart."

ISA. 35:6

"Go . . . and tell John . . . the lame walk."

LUKE 7:22

Look into our Lord's orthopaedic clinic, noting how he has made the lame man "leap as an hart." Examine closely the case histories.

1. He has treated and cured congenital deformity.
2. He has treated and cured those who suffer from a crippling caused by injury.
   a) Some such injuries are caused by the fault of others.
   b) Some are self-inflicted.
3. He has treated and cured those whose crippling has been caused by standing on an insecure foundation.
4. He has treated and cured those whose lameness may be characterized as a deficiency disease.

—John H. Withers, *Speak for Yourself*

417. THE HIGHWAY OF LIFE

"And an highway shall be there, and a way, and it shall be called the way of holiness." ISA. 35:8

1. It is a highway.
2. It is a safe way.
3. It is a direct way.
4. It is a friendly way.

—Hugh T. Kerr, *The Highway of Life*

418. THE ROYAL ROAD

"And an highway shall be there, and a way, and it shall be called The way of holiness; the unclean shall not pass over it; but it shall be for those: the wayfaring men, though fools, shall not err therein. No lion shall be there, nor any ravenous beast shall go up thereon, it shall not be found there; . . . And the ransomed of the Lord shall

*return, and come to Zion with songs and ever-
lasting joy upon their heads: they shall obtain joy
and gladness, and sorrow and sighing shall flee
away."*   ISA. 35:8-10

It is a distinctive mark of man that he makes
roads. No other creature does precisely that. But
God, the creator, has made a road too. Let us
look at it together.

  1. It is a highway.
      "An highway shall be there."
  2. It is a harmless way.
      "No lion shall be there, nor any ravenous
      beast."
  3. It is a happy way.
      "The ransomed of the Lord shall return,
      . . . with songs and everlasting joy."
  4. It is the homeward way.
      They shall "come to Zion."

419. THE GOSPEL HIGHWAY

Isa. 35:8-10

  1. The name on the way
      "The way of holiness"
  2. The people of the way
      "The ransomed of the Lord"
  3. The safety in the way
      "No lion shall be there, nor any ravenous
      beast."
  4. The ending of the way
      "Zion"

—David Hogg

420. THE RESIDUE OF LIFE

*"Mine age is departed, and is removed from me
as a shepherd's tent: I have cut off like a weaver
my life: he will cut me off with pining sickness."*
ISA. 38:12

This is part of a hymn made by a king who had
thought himself dying. These lines tell what
passed through his mind when, in the noontide
of his days, night seemed to be falling on him.

173

We, too, may have to undergo that experience and we, too, may put to ourselves questions like these:

1. What is left *from* my life?
   What remains of the past?
2. What is left *in* my life?
   Many things have had to go: what abides?
3. What is left *to* my life?
   How far have I yet to go?

—David Burns, *The Song of the Well*

421. TO THE DOUBTERS IN BABYLON

Isa. 40:12-31

1. Some said, "God has not the power."
   Reply: Our God made the world. (vss. 12-17) God packed the atom that man is now splitting.
2. Some said, "The graven images of Babylon are more powerful than Israel's God."
   Answer: Scorn on man-made images. (vss. 18-25)
3. Some said, "God has cast us off for our sin."
   Answer: God wearies not of his people. (vss. 26-28)
   Footnote: To know God's power, we must wait upon the Lord. (vss. 29-31)

—C. G. Wilkes

422. THE CHOSEN TREE

"*He that is so impoverished that he hath no oblation chooseth a tree that will not rot.*"

Isa. 40:20

1. The cross of Christ is called a tree.
2. The cross of Christ is a tree that will not rot.
3. The cross of Christ is a tree worthy of being chosen.
4. The cross of Christ is a tree chosen by the impoverished.

—James Smith, *Handfuls on Purpose*

423. THE RENEWED LIFE

"They that wait upon the Lord shall renew their strength: they shall mount up with wings as eagles; they shall run, and not be weary; and they shall walk, and not faint." Isa. 40:31

What sort of life is it? Let the text tell us:

1. It is a life without strain.
   "They shall mount up with wings as eagles."
2. It is a life without fatigue.
   "They shall run, and not be weary."
3. It is a life without cessation.
   "They shall walk, and not faint."
   —W. Y. Fullerton, *God's Highway*

424. SOMETHING TO GO HOME ON

"I the Lord have called thee in righteousness, and will hold thine hand, and will keep thee."
Isa. 42:6

Near Caswell Bay in South Wales stands a picturesque old house once the home of Frances Ridley Havergal. She had another home, however, to which she went from that very house. Shortly before her death, a friend, calling upon her, read to her this verse. The dying woman listened attentively, slowly repeating the words— "called," "held," "kept"; and then she added: "Well, I will just go home on that!"

It is a sure word to go home on. The Christian is:

1. Called
2. Held
3. Kept

425. WHEN GOD LOSES HIS MEMORY

"I . . . will not remember thy sins." Isa. 43:25

When human beings lose their memory, that is a sign of weakness; but when God loses his, it is a mark of strength. We forget because we cannot remember. He forgets because he will not remember.

175

1. It is fatal to forget the sin that God remembers.
   a) Jacob and Esau
   b) David and Bathsheba
   c) The pharisees and the woman taken in adultery
2. It is folly to remember the sin that God forgets.
3. It is only safe to forget the sin that God has forgotten.

426. GOD—BLOTTING OUT OUR SINS

"I, even I, am he that blotteth out thy transgressions for mine own sake, and will not remember thy sins." ISA. 43:25

Here are four beautiful thoughts about forgiven sins:

1. They are blotted out of God's book.
2. They are blotted out with God's hand.
   "It is the offended hand that blots them out." (Wilbur Chapman.)
3. They are blotted out for God's sake.
4. They are blotted out from God's memory.
   God remembers everything about you— except your forgiven sins!

—H. Grattan Guinness

427. BIOGRAPHY IN THREE WORDS

"Jacob my servant; and Israel, whom I have chosen . . . and thou, Jesurun, whom I have chosen." ISA. 44:1-2

Why were the chosen people called after Jacob rather than after Abraham or Isaac, both of whom seem to us worthier of the honor?

Perhaps it will help us to find an answer if we note that in this text he is given three names— Jacob, Israel, Jesurun. These denote a remarkable spiritual progress.

1. Jacob means supplanter.

2. Israel means contender with God.
3. Jesurun means straight or upright.

—James Stalker

428. FOUR GIRDINGS

1. The girding of overruling providence
   "I girded thee, though thou hast not known me." Isa. 45:5
2. The girding of conscious condescension
   "Jesus knowing that the Father had given all things into his hands, and that he was come from God, and went to God; He riseth from supper, and laid aside his garments; and took a towel, and girded himself." John 13:3, 4
3. The girding of compulsive circumstance
   "When thou wast young, thou girdedst thyself, and walkedst whither thou wouldest: but when thou shalt be old, thou shalt stretch forth thy hands, and another shall gird thee, and carry thee whither thou wouldest not." John 21:18
4. The girding of Christian character
   "Gird up the loins of your mind, be sober." I Pet. 1:13

429. WHY GOD HIDES HIMSELF

"Verily thou art a God that hidest thyself."

Isa. 45:15

Why does the divine Being thus remain invisible?

1. Because at our present stage of moral and spiritual development we could not bear the sight of his glorious personality.
2. Because the revelation for which we crave would be inconsistent with the divine modesty.
3. Because a disclosure of this kind would do away with the need for faith.
4. Because the time has not yet come for the full vision of God to be granted to us.

He hides Himself so wondrously,
    As if there were no God;
He is least seen when all the powers
    Of ill are most abroad.

—F. W. Faber

430. LIFE BY LOOKING

"*Look unto me, and be ye saved, all the ends of
the earth.*"   Isa. 45:22

  1. Sin came by a look.
        "When the woman saw that the tree was
        good for food."   Gen. 3:6
  2. Salvation comes by a look.
        "Look unto me, and be ye saved."
                                    Isa. 45:22
  3. Sanctification results from a look.
        "We all, with open face beholding as in
        a glass the glory of the Lord, are changed
        into the same image."   II Cor. 3:18
  4. Transformation will follow a look.
        "When he shall appear, we shall be like
        him."   I John 3:2

431. GOD CARRYING HIS PEOPLE

"*And even to your old age I am he; and even to
hoar hairs will I carry you.*"   Isa. 46:4

There are two ways of taking our religion. Let us
think of them together.

  1. The kind of religion that does nothing for
     us, but has to be carried as a burden.
  2. The other kind of religion, that can do some-
     thing for us, carry our burdens, and carry us.
                —D. M. Baillie, *Out of Nazareth*

432. THE DAWN OF THE DIVINE

"*He did say to me, My servant, art thou Israel,
in whom I shall break into glory?*"

        Isa. 49:3 George Adam Smith's Translation

God breaking into glory! That is a singular and
arresting idea. Not so do we normally think of

him. More often we conceive of his dwelling in glory than of his breaking into it. Yet such, according to the great expositor George Adam Smith, is the thought behind the verb translated "will be glorified" in the text. The suggestion is that through his servants God bursts upon the world like the unfolding of the dawn.

1. God breaks into glory in his servants when they proclaim his word.
2. God breaks into glory in his servants when they display his character.
3. God breaks into glory in his servants when for his sake they serve their fellow men.

433. THE GOD OF ALL COMFORT

1. Yesterday
   "The Lord hath comforted his people."
   Isa. 49:13

2. Today
   "I, am he that comforteth you."
   Isa. 51:12

3. Tomorrow
   "They shall be comforted." Matt. 5:4
   —Unknown

434. DIVINE DERMAGRAPHIA

"*Behold, I have graven thee upon the palms of my hands.*" Isa. 49:16

The practice of dermagraphia—or, to give it its simpler and more familiar name—"tattooing"—is nearly as old and as wide as the world. It was freely carried on in ancient times by the Japanese, the Maoris and the Picts or "painted men" of Scotland, and is still much in vogue with sailors, soldiers, and young men in general.

But who would ever have dreamed of associating such skin writing with God? Yet that is precisely what our text does.

"Behold, I have graven thee upon the palms of my hands." The words, originally addressed long ago to the people of Jerusalem, are applicable to

179

God's folk in all generations and in every land. To what do they point?

1. They point to a great grasp.

    Let me no more my comfort draw
    From my frail hold of Thee:
    In this alone rejoice with awe—
    Thy mighty grasp of me.

    Principal Shairp

2. They suggest a perfect knowledge.

    Of something that we know very well we say, "I know it like the palm of my hand." God knows us like that.

3. They hint at a shared pain.

    We are in the palm of his hand? Very well. The nail that pierced his hand will pierce us too.

435. GOD—THE REREWARD

"For ye shall not go out with haste, nor go by flight: for the Lord will go before you; and the God of Israel will be your rereward." Isa. 52:12

1. God our rereward means that the God of Israel will come between us and the sorrows of the past.

2. God our rereward means that the God of Israel will come between us and the sins of the past.

3. God our rereward means that the God of Israel stands by us ever counteracting the retrograde tendencies that we discover in ourselves.

4. God our rereward means that the God of Israel will save us from the special unknown perils of life.

5. God our rereward means that the God of Israel is mindful of the weakest of his people.

    —W. L. Watkinson, *The Blind Spot*

436. THE STARTLING CHRIST

"So shall he startle many nations."

Isa. 52:15 R.S.V.

"Say what you will," declared Pascal, "there is something in the Christian religion which is astonishing."

1. Christ was startling in his doctrine.
2. Christ was startling in his deeds.
3. Christ was startling in his death.

437. THE ARM OF THE LORD

"To whom is the arm of the Lord revealed?"

ISA. 53:1

1. It is revealed in creative power.
2. It is revealed in spiritual providence.
3. It is revealed in ruling purpose.
4. It is revealed in pastoral care.

—Ralph W. Sockman,
The Unemployed Carpenter

438. ALL WE LIKE SHEEP

"All we like sheep have gone astray; we have turned every one to his own way; and the Lord hath laid on him the iniquity of us all."

ISA. 53:6

We see here:

1. Universal depravity
   "All we like sheep have gone astray."
2. Individual perversity
   "We have turned every one to his own way."
3. Sacrificial sufficiency
   "And the Lord hath laid on him the iniquity of us all."

439. HOW IT HAS BEEN WITH US

ISA. 53:6.

Here we see:

1. Man's ruin
   "All we like sheep have gone astray."
2. Man's rebellion
   "We have turned every one to his own way."

181

3. Man's redemption
"And the Lord hath laid on him the iniquity of us all."

—Unknown

440. THE SICK CHRIST

Our first impulse is vehemently to protest against the very suggestion. Christ sick? Never. Not only was he never ill. He was and is a radiating center of health and healing.

Yet the Bible tells us of three things that made and make Christ sick.

1. He was made sick as a substitute for sin.
"Yet it pleased the Lord to bruise him; *he hath made him sick.*"

Isa. 53:10 R. V. Margin

2. He is made sick by his sympathy for sufferers.
"I was sick, and ye visited me."

Matt. 25:36

3. He is made sick by the half-heartedness of his people.
"So then because thou art lukewarm, and neither cold nor hot, I will spew thee out of my mouth." Rev. 3:16

441. PROGENY OF JESUS

"He shall see his seed." Isa. 53:10

Jesus founded no family. In this he differed from most of the great moral teachers of mankind— Confucius, Buddha, Mohammed. Yet here is the prophet predicting that he shall see his seed. What does he mean? He is speaking of Christ's spiritual family.

"He shall see his seed."

1. He shall see them born and brought in.
2. He shall see them educated and brought up.
3. He shall see them supported and brought through.
4. He shall see them transported and brought home.

442. THE CHEAPEST MARKET

"Ho, every one that thirsteth, come ye to the waters, and he that hath no money; come ye, buy, and eat; yea, come, buy wine and milk without money and without price." Isa. 55:1

1. The articles for sale
     "Wine and milk"
         a. Milk emblematic of that which contains all the essentials of life
         b. Wine emblematic of that which cheers and inspires.
2. The price to be paid
     "Without money and without price"
3. The customers invited
         a. The thirsty
             "Ho, everyone that thirsteth"
         b. The bankrupt
             "He that hath no money"

     —James Smith, *Handfuls on Purpose*

443. THE "OH" AND THE "HO"

"Ho, every one that thirsteth, come ye to the waters, and he that hath no money; come ye, buy, and eat; yea, come, buy wine and milk without money and without price." Isa. 55:1

Evangelism at its best is the "oh" of delighted discovery of Christ turned into the "ho" of impassioned invitation to Christ.

Note:

1. It is a loud call.
     You do not say "ho" in a whisper.
2. It is a personal call.
     Uttered by a person, it is addressed to a person.
3. It is a universal call.
     "Every one."
4. It is an individual call.
     "Every one."
5. It is a conditional call.
     "That thirsteth."

444. WEBS OR GARMENTS?

"Their webs shall not become garments."

ISA. 59:6

1. Let us ask whether the webs of modern industry are being finished off into garments for the people.
2. Let us ask whether our educational system is a web failing to become a garment when it makes men clever without making them good.
3. Let us ask whether the web of our ecclesiastical organization is failing to become a garment when it does not produce mature Christian character.

—Rees Griffiths, *The Reserves of the Soul*

445. FLOODS

Floods can bring fertility or fatality. They can enrich or they can destroy. They can be a blessing or a curse.

Think of the seasonal flooding of the Nile and of the prosperity which it brings to Egypt. Think, too, of the disastrous Mississippi floods of February—July, 1927. And think of the terrible floods of the River Assiniboine in 1950.

So with spiritual floods. Consider:

1. The flood of temptation
   "When the adversary shall come in like a flood, the spirit of the Lord shall lift up a standard against him."

   Isa. 59:19 R. V. Margin
2. The flood of trial
   "He is like a man building a house, who dug deep, and laid the foundation upon rock; and when a flood arose, the stream broke against that house, and could not shake it, because it had been well built."

   Luke 6:48 R. S. V.
3. The flood of revival
   "I will pour water upon him that is thirsty,

and floods upon the dry ground."

Isa. 44:3

446. DOVES TO THEIR WINDOWS

"Who are these that fly as a cloud, and as the doves to their windows?" Isa. 60:8

How do doves fly?

1. They fly low.
2. They fly for shelter.
3. They fly home.
4. They fly in flocks.

—T. De Witt Talmage

447. WHY THE SPIRIT INSPIRES A PREACHER

"The Spirit of the Lord God is upon me, because. . ." Isa. 61:1 R.S.V.

There is always a reason for the divine endowment. What is it?

To bring the following fourfold blessing:

1. A passing from want to wealth
   "Good tidings to the afflicted." This means that sin is poverty and salvation riches.
2. A passing from hurt to healing
   "To bind up the brokenhearted."
   This suggests that sin is sickness and salvation health.
3. A passing from fetters to freedom.
   "Liberty to the captives, and the opening of the prison to those who are bound."
   This implies that sin is bondage and salvation liberty.
4. Opening of the eyes
   "The recovering of sight to the blind."
   This intimates that sin is sightlessness and salvation seeing.

448. FADING AWAY

"We all do fade as a leaf." Isa. 64:6

How does a leaf fade?

1. By a necessary law
2. By a gradual process
3. Into its primitive element
4. Preparatory to a new life
5. As a progressive stage of life

—David Thomas

449. AS A LEAF

"We all do fade as a leaf." ISA. 64:6

This means that we fade:

1. Not alone.
2. Not until the time comes.
3. Not without beauty.
4. Not without purposed productivity.

—Unknown

450. THE GOD OF THE AMEN

"He who blesseth himself in the earth shall bless himself in the God of [the Amen]."

ISA. 65:16

1. Note the meaning of the name—strong, firm, true, reliable.
2. Note how this God of the Amen is, for that very reason, the source of all blessing.
3. Note how the God of the Amen should be the pattern of his servants.

—Alexander Maclaren, *The God of the Amen*

451. THE THREE VOICES

"A voice of noise from the city, a voice from the temple, a voice of the Lord." ISA. 66:6

1. The voice of society
2. The voice of the church
3. The voice of the Lord

452. GOD LIKE A MOTHER

"As one whom his mother comforteth, so will I comfort you." ISA. 66:13

Note that:

1. Like a mother, God gives us his life.
2. Like a mother, God gives us his love.
3. Like a mother, God gives us his labor.
4. Like a mother, God gives us his likeness.

453. THE MOTHERLINESS OF GOD

"As one whom his mother comforteth, so will I comfort you." Isa. 66:13

"As a mother"—why?

1. Because his comforts are effectual in circumstances where no one else can succeed.
2. Because his comforts are applicable to troubles in which no one else is interested.
3. Because his comforts are expressed in forms which no one else can make efficient.

—Thomas Davies, *Sermonic Studies*

JEREMIAH

454. FOUNTAIN OR CISTERN

"My people have committed two evils; they have forsaken me the fountain of living waters, and hewed them out cisterns, broken cisterns, that can hold no water." JER. 3:13

Note the difference between them:

1. A cistern is artificial, a fountain is natural.
2. A cistern is static, a fountain is living.
3. A cistern evaporates, a fountain flows on forever.

455. REASONS FOR RETURNING

JER. 3:12, 14, 22

1. An unchanged character
"Return . . . for I am merciful."

2. An unaltered relationship
   "Turn . . . I am married unto you."
3. An unfailing promise
   "Return . . . I will heal your backslidings."
   —Henry Pickering

456. WHEN THINGS GO AGAINST YOU— WHAT THEN?

"When thou art spoiled, what wilt thou do?"
JER. 4:30

1. Rebel?
2. Resign?
3. Rebuild?

457. IN COMPANY WITH THE GREAT

"I will get me unto the great men." JER. 5:5

1. That will make me grateful.
   Wherefore praise we famous men,
   From whose bays we borrow—
   They that put aside today,
   All the joys of their today,
   And with the toil of their today
   Bought for us tomorrow?
2. That will make me humble.
3. That will make me inspired.

458. THE HABITS OF MIGRANTS

"Yea, the stork in the heaven knoweth her appointed times; and the turtle and the crane and the swallow observe the time of their coming; but my people know not the judgment of the Lord."
JER. 8:7

1. They mingle music with their flight.
   Migrants fly singing.
2. They fly very high.
3. They know when to start.

—T. De Witt Talmage

459. MIGRATION

"Yea, the stork in the heaven knoweth her appointed times; and the turtle and the crane and

the swallow observe the time of their coming;
but my people know not the judgment of the
Lord." JER. 8:7

Among all the marvels of nature none is more
mysterious or more fascinating than the migratory
instinct in certain types of bird.

Why do the winged tribes thus wing their way
across the width of the world? Naturalists assign
various causes. Some say they go in search of
food. Some say they go to mate and rear their
young. But surely the most obvious reason is that
they go because they have the wit to dodge the
winter.

They go before the storms break—an instinct
which, according to our text, the people of God
do not always possess.

There are three sorts of migration which have
sometimes to be undertaken at the bidding of the
divine.

1. Geographical migration
   Think of Abram, Lot, the children of Israel, the Huguenots, the Pilgrims, and so
   on.

2. Moral migration
   It may not always be necessary for the
   Christian to get out of some compromising
   situation, but it will always be needful to
   get it out of him.

3. Eternal migration
   It is said that swallows, born in captivity
   and kept in tiny cages, become strangely
   agitated and excited when the migratory
   season commences. So with the Christian.
   A compelling instinct urges him to seek a
   better world.

460. THE WINTER OF THE SOUL

"The harvest is past, the summer is ended, and
we are not saved." JER. 8:20

1. Summer is a preparation for winter.
2. Winter comes rapidly upon us.

3. When winter sets in harvest cannot be recalled.

—W. E. LEE

461. BALM IN GILEAD

"Is there no balm in Gilead?" JER. 8:22
Note:

1. This balm was derived from a tree.

   What balm streams from the Cross! "The medicine here referred to is a resinous substance obtained from the balsam tree, which flourished near Gilead, and was far-famed for its healing properties, often sold for twice its weight in silver. It was obtained by cutting the bark with an axe when the fresh juices were most vigorous. The quantity which exuded from one tree did not exceed sixty drops a day."

2. This balm was exceedingly precious.

   "Sold for twice its weight in silver."

3. The balm possessed marvelous healing properties.

   But—it had to be applied!

462. WHAT TO BOAST ABOUT

"Let not the wise man glory in his wisdom, neither let the mighty man glory in his might, let not the rich man glory in his riches: But let him that glorieth glory in this, that he understandeth and knoweth me, that I am the Lord." JER. 9:23-24

1. Let not the wise man glory in his wisdom.
2. Let not the mighty man glory in his might.
3. Let not the rich man glory in his riches.
4. But he that glorieth, let him glory in this, that he understandeth and knoweth me, that I am the Lord.

—Unknown

463. THE SWELLING OF JORDAN

"If thou hast run with the footmen, and they have wearied thee, then how canst thou contend

with horses? and if in the land of peace, wherein
thou trustedst, they wearied thee, then how wilt
thou do in the swelling of Jordan?"   JER. 12:5

Consider:

1. The swelling Jordan of doubt.
2. The swelling Jordan of temptation.
3. The swelling Jordan of sorrow.
4. The swelling Jordan of death.

464. THE PARABLE OF THE POTTER

JER. 18:1-23

1. The prophet
   a. His perplexity
   b. His perception
2. The potter
   a. His material
   b. His method
3. The parable
   a. The compassion of God
   b. The mode of salvation
4. The pitcher
   a. Its making
   b. Its marring
   c. Its remaking

—David Hogg

465. SEEING LIFE WHOLE

"Arise, and go down to the potter's house, and
there I will cause thee to hear my words. Then
I went down to the potter's house, and, behold,
he wrought a work on the wheels. And the vessel
that he made of clay was marred in the hand of
the potter: so he made it again another vessel, as
seemed good to the potter to make it."

JER. 18:2-4

Jeremiah saw five things in the potter's shop. Not
all do.

1. Some see only the clay.
       The crude stuff of our human nature.
2. Some see only the wheel.

3. Some see the potter's shaping hand.
4. Some see the fire.
5. Some see the finished work of art.

—James Black

466. THE PARABLE IN THE POTTERY

"Arise, and go down to the potter's house, and there I will cause thee to hear my words. Then I went down to the potter's house, and, behold, he wrought a work on the wheels. And the vessel that he made of clay was marred in the hand of the potter; so he made it again another vessel, as seemed good to the potter to make it."

JER. 18:2-4

1. Formed
   "He wrought a work on the wheels."
2. Deformed
   "The vessel . . . was marred in the hand of the potter."
3. Reformed
   "He made it again."

467. THE SUCCESS THAT IS FAILURE

"Woe unto him that buildeth his house by unrighteousness." JER. 22:13

If I were a Christian businessman, I would be a Christian first and a businessman afterwards. I would not encourage the legalizing of wrong, even if I believed it helped business, and I would pay my assistants what they earned and deserved.

1. Building by unrighteous trade
   For example, various forms of fraud
2. Building by oppression of employees
   Frequent payment of living wage and fair distribution of profits
3. Building by unjust administration of laws.
   Favoring the rich—"the law's delay"

Application: "Woe unto him."

—M. B. Tanner

468. THE PATENT OF NOBILITY

"The princes of Judah, with the carpenters and smiths, from Jerusalem." JER. 24:1

Nebuchadnezzar carried away with him all the great men: he left the common people. He took the aristocracy; namely, the princes, with the carpenters and smiths.

Learn indirectly the nobility of work and the high rank of every true servant of the community.

1. Labor is noble when regarded as the service of God.
2. Labor is noble as it becomes a social service.
3. Labor is noble as it becomes an education of our highest nature.

—W. L. Watkinson,
The Education of the Heart

469. LIVING ACCORDING TO PLAN

"The plans which I am planning for you."
JER. 29:11 J. B. Rotherham

God's plan for us is:

1. A predetermined plan.
2. A gradually unfolded plan.
3. A plan apart from conformity to which life, however successful by human standards, is ultimately utter loss.

470. WAYMARKS

"Set thee up waymarks." JER. 31:21

1. Waymarks serve as a spur to memory.
2. Waymarks act as a stimulus to gratitude.
3. Waymarks map out the track for those who come after.

471. GOD—A HUSBAND

"I was an husband unto them." JER. 31:32

The word "husband" is very interesting. It is a corruption of "house-band"—the one who holds the house together.

193

Think how God stands in that relation to his people.

1. The husband is responsible for bringing the household into existence.
2. The husband is responsible for supporting the household.
3. The husband communicates his image to the members of the household.

472. HOW SIN IS FINISHED WITH

"I will forgive their iniquity, and I will remember their sin no more." JER. 31:34

1. Sin is not finished with when it is forsaken.
2. Sin is not finished with when it is forgotten.
3. Sin is not finished with when it is forgiven by the human beings who have been hurt by it.
4. Sin is only finished with when it is forgiven and forgotten by God.

Faber wrote:

> Have you sinned as none else in the world did before you?
> Are you blacker than all other creatures in guilt?
> Oh, fear not; oh, doubt not—the mother who bore you
> Loves you less than the Saviour whose blood you have spilt.

473. THE ROAD TO RUIN

"Thy friends have set thee on, and have prevailed against thee: thy feet are sunk in the mire, and they are turned away back." JER. 38:22

We are reminded by these words:

1. That men have the power of "setting each other on" in evil ways.
2. That those who seek to do this all too often succeed.
3. That those who so succeed generally land themselves in difficulties.

4. That those who thus involve others in difficulties usually leave them in the lurch.

—Thomas Davies, Sermonic Studies

474. THE FALLACY OF BIGNESS

"Seekest thou great things for thyself? seek them not." JER. 45:5

Great things are not necessary:

1. For the production of great character.
2. For the conception of great ideas.
3. For the doing of great service.

Adapted.
—W. L. Watkinson,
The Education of the Heart

475. DON'T SETTLE DOWN

"Moab . . . hath settled on his lees."
JER. 48:11

If wine were left too long in one vessel, the sediment would spoil its flavor. It had to be emptied from one vessel to another. Too settled a life is a thoroughly bad thing.

Are we sometimes in danger of becoming "settled upon our lees?"

1. This is a challenge to our mind.
2. This is a challenge to our conscience.
3. This is a challenge to our will.

—John B. Nettleship

476. DWELL DEEP

"Dwell deep." JER. 49.8

1. Dwell deep in doctrine.
2. Dwell deep in devotion.
3. Dwell deep in dedication.

477. ASKING THE WAY

"They shall ask the way to Zion with their faces thitherward." JER. 50:5

1. Ask the way because it can be known.

2. Ask the way because you do not know it.
3. Ask the way because, if you ask aright, you cannot fail of an answer.

478. LETTING THE CHURCH COME INTO YOUR MIND

"*Remember the Lord afar off, and let Jerusalem come into your mind.*" JER. 51:50

1. Let the Church come into your mind to join its fellowship.
2. Let the Church come into your mind to pray for it.
3. Let the church come into your mind to give to it.
4. Let the Church come into your mind to work for it.

—John McIlveen,
Christ and the Christian Life

LAMENTATIONS

479. THE COMPONENTS OF DIVINE COMPASSION

"*Because his compassions fail not.*" LAM. 3:22

1. The first great attribute in compassion is the understanding mind.
2. The second great attribute of compassion is magnanimity.
3. The third great attribute of compassion is re-creative moral power.

—George A. Gordon, *Great Modern Sermons*

480. MORNING MERCIES

"*They are new every morning.*" LAM. 3:23
This speaks of:

1. The freshness of God's mercies.
2. The brightness of God's mercies.
3. The unchangeableness of God's mercies.
4. The promptness of God's mercies.

481. GOODNESS IS GOOD FOR YOU

1. The goodness of deliverance
   "It is good that a man should both hope and quietly wait for the salvation of the Lord."   Lam. 3:26
2. The goodness of discipline
   "It is good for a man that he should bear the yoke in his youth."   Lam. 3:27
3. The goodness of distress
   "It is good for me that I have been afflicted."   Ps. 119:71
4. The goodness of devotion
   "It is good for me to draw near to God."
   Ps. 73:28

482. YOUTH AND THE YOKE

"It is good for a man that he bear the yoke in his youth."   LAM. 3:27
Why?

1. Because then he is best able to carry it.
2. Because then he may most easily grow accustomed to it.
3. Because then he will most be tempted to revolt against it.
   But consider Christ's declaration: "My yoke is easy."   Matt. 11:30

483. THE EYE AND THE HEART

"Mine eye affecteth mine heart."   LAM. 3:51
We are embodied spirits. We are each shut up in our house of flesh, and the eye is the window through which we look out. As we gaze forth we undergo an endless impression, impulse and alteration. Our eye affects our heart. Note:

1. Mine eye affecteth my heart to spoil it.
2. Mine eye affecteth my heart to cleanse it.

3. Mine eye affecteth my heart to thrill it.
4. Mine eye affecteth my heart to save it.
—David Burns, *The Song of the Well*

EZEKIEL

484. THE FOUR FACES OF THE CHRISTIAN

"As for the likeness of their faces, they four had the face of a man, and the face of a lion, on the right side: and they four had the face of an ox on the left side; they four also had the face of an eagle." EZEK. 1:10

To call a person "two-faced" is by no means to pay him a compliment. Yet here is the prophet Ezekiel speaking of four great messengers of God as each possessing four faces:

Every Christian should be four-faced, many-sided, capable, and versatile.

1. He should have in him the ox element:
   patience, industry, tractability.
2. He should have in him the lion element:
   strength, boldness
3. He should have the eagle element:
   buoyancy, vision.
4. He should have the man element:
   intelligence, sympathy, sanctity.

—J. Ossian Davies, *The Dayspring*

485. THE WHISPERING CHAMBERS OF THE IMAGINATION

"Son of man, have you seen what the elders of the house of Israel are doing in the dark, every man in his room of pictures?" EZEK. 8:12 R.S.V.

1. Imagination is the control room of health.
2. Imagination is the creative center of life.

3. Imagination is the citadel of the soul.
—John H. Withers, *Speak for Yourself*

486. THE PRIVATE PICTURE GALLERY

"Every man is his room of pictures."

EZEK. 8:12

1. Every man's imagination is a picture gallery.
2. The pictures displayed in that gallery make him what he is.
3. What sort of pictures are on the walls of our galleries?

487. STANDING IN THE GAP

"I sought for a man among them, that should . . . stand in the gap before me for the land."

EZEK. 22:30

1. Young men are needed to stand in the gap caused by the passing on of those of an older generation.
2. Men are required to stand in the gap created by the widespread secession of people from the churches.
3. Men are called for to stand in the gap brought about by secular assaults on the faith.

488. GOVERNOR AMONG THE NATIONS

EZEK. 29:17-20

From this passage we learn that:

1. The disposal of states or nations is the work of God.
2. Men can serve God without being aware of it.
3. None can be losers in what they do for God.

—William Henry Young,
How to Preach with Power

489. SHOWERS OF BLESSING

"There shall be showers of blessing."

EZEK. 34:26

1. Rain softens the hard soil.
2. Rain ripens the crop.
3. Rain gladdens the husbandman.

—J. T. Tucker

490. THE OUTLOOK OF THE OPTIMIST

"I . . . will do better unto you than at your beginnings."   EZEK. 36:11

1. There is an optimism that is temperamental.
2. There is a shallow optimism which is happy because half-blind.
3. There is a prophetic optimism which knows that beneath all change are the arms of the everlasting God.

—G. H. Morrison,
The Incomparable Christ

491. THE HEART OF STONE

"I will take away the stony heart out of your flesh."   EZEK. 36:26

This suggests that:

1. The heart is as cold as a stone.
2. The heart is as dead as a stone.
3. The heart is as insensible as a stone.

—Thomas Guthrie

492. VALOR IN THE VALLEY

"Can these bones live?"   EZEK. 37:3

What a reversal we have in this narrative of the normal fate of an army! Man begins with an army and ends with bones: God here begins with bones and ends with an army.

Perhaps the main points in the story can be best brought out by three words:

1. The bones
2. The breath
3. The battalion

493. THE VISION IN THE VALLEY

"And he said unto me, Son of man, can these bones live? And I answered, O Lord God, thou knowest." Ezek. 37:3

This is an age of vision. In our day man has by mechanical means vastly extended the range of his faculty of sight. For instance, X rays, microscopes, telescopes, and so forth.

But is this an age of spiritual vision? Few would say it was.

1. The bones—a proof of extinct life.
     a. Very many
     b. Very dry
     c. Very disorderly
     d. Very exposed
2. The breath—an evidence of available life.
3. The battalion—a manifestation of ordered, organized, militant life.

494. MEASURING THE RIVER

"And when the man that had the line in his hand went forth eastward, he measured a thousand cubits, and he brought me through the waters; the waters were to the ancles. Again he measured a thousand, and brought me through the waters; the waters were to the knees. Again he measured a thousand, and brought me through; the waters were to the loins. Afterward he measured a thousand; and it was a river that I could not pass over: for the waters were risen, waters to swim in, a river that could not be passed over."

Ezek. 47:3-5

1. Measuring to the ankles—that speaks of the Christian's walk.
2. Measuring to the knees—that speaks of the Christian's devotional life.
3. Measuring to the loins—that speaks of the Christian's purity and service.
4. Measuring to swimming depth—that speaks of the Christian's ample resources.

DANIEL

495. THE IMAGE AND THE FURNACE
Dan. 3:11-17

1. Bow or burn—the despot's decree.
2. Burn, not bow—the heroes' resolution.
3. Neither bow nor burn—the Lord's decision.

—John A. Kern,
The Ministry to the Congregation

496. THE MATTER THAT MATTERS
"*We are not careful to answer thee in this matter.*"
Dan. 3:16

Philip Jones, a famous Welsh preacher of a former day, once preached on this text. Having announced it, he suddenly broke out: "What matter?" A prolonged pause. Then a thunderous shout: "The matter that matters!"

It was indeed. Note that:

1. It was a matter of right or wrong.
2. It was a matter of God or man.
3. It was a matter of life or death.

497. FAITH'S FINAL WORD
"*But if not . . . we will not.*" Dan. 3:18
Here is:

1. Heroic adherence to high principle.
2. Humble submission to the will of God.
3. Hearty contempt of threatened consequences.

—John Pollock,
The Farther Horizon

498. THE WRITING ON THE WALL
"*In the same hour came forth the fingers of a man's hand, and wrote over against the candlestick upon the plaster of the wall of the king's palace: and the king saw the part of the hand that wrote.*" Dan. 5:5

1. There is a hand silently writing our history.
2. This inscription is always being penned.
3. One day the writing will confront us.
4. The only way to blot out the writing is to have it nailed to the cross of Christ.

—W. E. Lee

499. IN THE BALANCE

"Thou art weighed in the balances, and art found wanting." DAN. 5:27

I watched a man and his wife standing by a weighing machine in a large department store not long ago. The woman got on the scales. But not until she had divested herself of most of her clothing, handing the articles of dress to her husband one by one until I thought she was planning to go on the machine wearing only a bathing costume! You see, there were many people looking on and she wished to appear to advantage on the scales! I wonder how we look on God's scales! There are several balances in which men are morally weighed:

1. The balance of Holy Scripture
2. The balance of conscience
3. The balance of circumstances
4. The balance of public opinion
5. But what finally signifies is the balance of divine judgment

500. CAROUSEL

"In that night was Belshazzar the king of the Chaldeans slain." DAN. 5:30

1. When God writes anything on the wall a man had better read it as it is.
2. There is a great difference between the opening of the banquet of sin and its close.
3. Death sometimes breaks in upon a banquet.
4. The destruction of those who despise God will be very sudden.

—T. De Witt Talmage

501. ALONE WITH GOD

"I was left alone, and saw this great vision."

DAN. 10:8

What is it to be alone? The etymology of the word provides a clue. To be "alone" is to be "all one." Hence to be "alone" with God is to be "all one" with him.

Such solitude begets great visions.

1. The vision of divine holiness
2. The vision of personal unworthiness
3. The vision of social usefulness

502. STAR PREACHERS

"They that turn many to righteousness [shall shine] as the stars for ever and ever."

DAN. 12:3

How do the stars shine?

1. They shine when it is dark.
2. They shine steadfastly.
3. They shine modestly.
4. They shine everlastingly.

HOSEA

503. DIVINE DOWNPOUR

"That He may come upon us like a downpour, like the harvest rain and the seed rain of the land."

Hos. 6:3 J. B. Rotherham

The Bible speaks of the rain in three ways.

1. Rain as a minister of judgment
2. Rain as a test of moral quality.
3. Rain as a bringer of divine blessing.

Adapted.

—F. E. Marsh, *Emblems of the Holy Spirit*

504. VANISHING VIRTUE

"*Your goodness is as a morning cloud, and as the early dew it goeth away.*"   Hos. 6:4

1. Some people's virtue vanishes because it is merely sentimental.
2. Some people's virtue vanishes because it is simply theoretical.
3. Some people's virtue vanishes because it is too exclusively personal.

505. OVERDONE AND UNDERDONE

"*Ephraim is a cake not turned.*"   Hos. 7:8

We are all interested in the art of cooking. The preparation of food is one of the most important departments of domestic economy. But a discussion of the art of cooking does not come within the scope of my purpose. I desire rather to take the prophet's illustration concerning Ephraim and apply it to the religious life of the present time.

Let me point out to you some of the unturned cakes that are too often found within the bounds of all our congregations.

Some have:

1. Orthodoxy without life.
2. Piety without principle.
3. Morality without religion.
4. Zeal without knowledge.
5. Enthusiasm without faithfulness.
6. Desire without decision.

—W. W. Weeks, *The Face of Christ*

506. WHEN GREAT THINGS ARE COUNTED STRANGE THINGS

"*I have written to him the great things of my law, but they were counted a strange thing.*"
Hos. 8:12

Great things are counted strange things:

1. When we have grown accustomed to mediocrity.

2. When we have mislaid the power of magnetic expectancy.
3. When we have lost sight of the greatness of God.

507. FALLOW GROUND
"Break up your fallow ground." Hos. 10:12

1. It is sometimes good for ground to lie fallow for a while.
2. Nevertheless, fallow ground is unfruitful ground.
3. There is a season for breaking up the fallow ground.
   a) The fallow ground of the mind needs breaking up with the share of fresh truth.
   b) The fallow ground of the soul needs breaking up with the plough of prayer.
   c) The fallow ground of the unevangelized world needs breaking up with the coulter of the gospel.

508. THE DRAWINGS OF THE DIVINE
"I drew them with cords of a man, with bands of love." Hos. 11:4

1. The prophet with a broken heart.
2. The God with a broken heart
3. The sin against love
4. The love which conquers sin

—Lynn Harold Hough

509. SINCE GOD IS NOT MAN
"I am God, and not man." Hos. 11:9

Here a truth which in our day needs to be shouted from the housetops. In our efforts to understand God, we have pulled him down to our level, and made him in our image. We need a fresh emphasis on the truth that God is God and not man.

What follows from this?

1. Because God is God and not man, he is changeless.
2. Because God is God and not man, he has infinite faith in people.
3. Because God is God and not man, he is uncompromising in his hatred of sin.
4. Because God is God and not man, his love and patient forbearance are exhaustless.

—W. M. Elliott, Jr.

510. VERBAL APPROACH TO THE DIVINE
"Take with you words, and turn to the Lord."
Hos. 14:2

God can read the heart, but he nevertheless likes to hear the utterance of the lips. So, as you enter his presence, obey the prophetic injunction and take with you words.

1. Take with you words of penitence.
2. Take with you words of petition.
3. Take with you words of praise.

511. GOD AS THE DEW
"I will be as the dew unto Israel." Hos. 14:5

Note the following facts about dew:

1. It is heavenly in its origin.
2. It is condensed in the stillness.
3. It is beautifying in its effect.
4. It is fructifying in its operation.

512. THE DEW
"I will be as the dew unto Israel." Hos. 14:5

1. Dew forms in the dark.
2. Dew comes in the calm.
3. Dew distils silently.
4. Dew promotes growth.

513. GOD AS THE DEW
"I will be as the dew unto Israel." Hos. 14:5
This means that:

1. God is the satisfier of our spiritual thirst.
2. God blesses us in the night season.
3. God's is a blessing which comes in needful proportions.
4. As the dew forms in different quantities upon different substances under precisely similar conditions, so our measure of God and his blessings is determined by the disposition of our spirits.

—E. Aubrey

514. SPIRITUAL STRENGTH

"And cast forth his roots as Lebanon." Hos. 14:5

Several thoughts are here suggested to our mind:

1. Spiritual strength is primarily an invisible growth.
2. Spiritual strength is ours in proportion to our inner response to the divine.
3. Spiritual strength is seen in unwavering steadfastness.

—E. Aubrey

515. GROWING AS THE VINE

"And grow as the vine." Hos. 14:7

How does the vine grow? To what sort of growth does this refer?

1. It is growth in dependence upon superior strength.
2. It is growth in an elevated situation.
3. It is growth by purging and pruning.
4. It is growth of which fruitfulness is the purposed end.

—E. Aubrey

JOEL

516. THREE RENDINGS

"Rend your heart, and not your garments, and turn unto the Lord your God: for he is gracious and merciful, slow to anger, and of great kindness, and repenteth him of the evil. Who knoweth if he will return and repent, and leave a blessing behind him?" JOEL 2:13-14

1. The rent habit
    "Not your garments."
2. The rent heart
    "Rend your heart."
3. The rent heaven
    "Who knoweth if he will return and repent, and leave a blessing behind him?"

517. THE POWER OF POSITIVE THINKING

"Let the weak say, I am strong." JOEL 3:10

There are several ways in which a man might say this.

He might say it:

1. In foolish self-ignorance.
2. In presumptuous pretence.
3. In mere autosuggestion.
4. But he might say it also in the optimism which is born of a living faith in God.

AMOS

518. THE WINDS OF GOD

"[He] createth the wind." AMOS 4:13

Mankind has ever been interested in the winds.

Hygiene, agriculture, and navigation need them. The purifying of the atmosphere of noxious vapors, the propagation of millions of seeds, the transportation of the clouds—all demonstrate how dependent man is upon the winds.

Four great winds are mentioned in the Bible and each has its own special significance.

1. The north wind speaks of the testings of God.
2. The south wind speaks of the goodness of God.
3. The east wind speaks of the judgments of God.
4. The west wind speaks of the mercy of God.

—A. W. Clines

519. THE GREAT INTERVIEW

"Prepare to meet thy God." AMOS 4:12

There are some persons we never meet. Thousands of miles divide us. We never will meet them in house or store or street. But God we must meet.

1. We must meet God in the misfortunes of life.
2. We must meet God in the bereavements of of life.
3. We must meet God in the hour of death.
4. We must meet God in the great Day.

—T. De Witt Talmage

520. GOD'S PLUMBLINE

"Thus he shewed me: and, behold, the Lord stood upon a wall made by a plumbline, with a plumbline in his hand. And the Lord said unto me, Amos, what seest thou? And I said, A plumbline. Then said the Lord, Behold, I will set a plumbline in the midst of my people Israel: I will not again pass by them any more." AMOS 7:7-8

This suggests:

1. God's accuracy in building nature.
2. God's standard for testing character.

3. God's method of destroying evil.
—Daniel Hughes, *The Making of Man*

OBADIAH

521. THE NONSENSE OF NEUTRALITY

"*In the day that thou stoodest on the other side, even thou wast as one of them.*" OBAD. 11

The book of Obadiah is like the apostle Paul, very small but also very full of fire. There is only one chapter in it, and that chapter has only twenty-one verses, but every word is like a hammer blow, and every sentence cuts.

What the author is tilting against all through is the sin of neutrality.

1. It is a sin against self.
2. It is a sin against society.
3. It is a sin against God.

—D. C. Mitchell,
The Nonsense of Neutrality

JONAH

522. JONAH'S FARE

"*He [Jonah] paid the fare thereof.*" JONAH 1:3

1. Jonah paid the fare for his proud exclusiveness.
2. Jonah paid the fare for his personal disobedience of God.
3. Jonah paid the fare for his private delusions.

—John H. Withers, *Speak for Yourself*

MICAH

523. THE GOD WHO COMES DOWN

"For, behold, the Lord cometh forth out of his place, and will come down." MIC. 1:3

In Morley's monumental Life of William Ewart Gladstone, a comical little episode is recorded. A deputation had called at No. 10, Downing Street to ask for the help of the great prime minister with a social problem. Gladstone was busy in an upstairs apartment when they arrived and, until he should be free to see them, his wife entertained the deputation downstairs. Being so full of their troubles, they began to pour them out to her, the spokesman at last ending the long recital with the pious ejaculation: "Well, anyway, there's One above who will be able to put everything right!" Mistaking their meaning, Mrs. Gladstone replied: "Yes, he'll be down any minute now!"

This incident strikes the keynote for a sermon on our text: "For, behold, the Lord cometh forth out of his place, and will come down."

The Bible tells us that God came down on three tremendous occasions.

> 1. He came down with the law of life.
>   On Sinai
> 2. He came down with the gift of life.
>   At Bethlehem
> 3. He came down with the power for life.
>   At Pentecost

524. THE BREAKER

"The breaker is come before them."

MIC. 2:13

Observe that the word here used signifies:

> 1. A breaking forth
> 2. A breaking down
> 3. A breaking through
>   —Daniel Hughes, *The Making of Man*

212

525. SPEARS AND PRUNINGHOOKS

"They shall beat their . . . spears into pruning-hooks." Mic. 4:3

We have here:

1. A comparison.

   Both spears and pruninghooks are made of metal, of the same metal. Note: earth's raw materials are neither good nor bad, save as we make them so.

2. A contrast.

   The spear is a weapon of war, the pruninghook an implement of peace.

3. A conversion.

   Spears *into* pruninghooks. The spears were not to be destroyed: they were to be transformed. It was to be a process of sublimation.

526. GOINGS FORTH AND COMING FORTH

"But thou, Bethlehem Ephratah, though thou be little among the thousands of Judah, yet out of thee shall he come forth unto me that is to be ruler in Israel: whose goings forth have been from of old, from everlasting." Mic. 5:2

Consider:

1. The goings forth of the eternal Christ and the coming forth of the historic Jesus.
2. The going forth of creative power and the coming forth of redemptive love.
3. The going forth of the Lord of the past and the coming forth of the Lord of the future.

527. WHY WE MUST NOT WORSHIP THE WORK OF OUR OWN HANDS

"Thou shalt no more worship the work of thine own hands." Mic. 5:13

On a higher level than that of primitive idolatry this is the besetting sin of modern man. He worships the work of his own hands—his scientific inventions, his technological skills, his practical

213

achievements in the realms of architecture, engineering, and so on.

Yet here we are expressly forbidden to worship the work of our own hands.

Why?

1. Because when we worship the work of our own hands, we are bowing down to something less than ourselves. This is always debasing.

2. Because when we worship the work of our own hands, we are merely doing obeisance to an extension of ourselves. This is perilous pride.

3. Because when we worship the work of our own hands, we are prostrating ourselves before something which is powerless to help us at the point of our sorest need.

528. THE SUMMING UP

"What doth the Lord require of thee, but to do justly, and to love mercy, and to walk humbly with thy God?" Mic. 6:8

1. Our relation to those around us
   "Do justly."
2. Our relation to those beneath us
   "Love mercy."
3. Our relation to the One above us
   "Walk humbly with thy God."

NAHUM

529. FAIR FEET

"Behold upon the mountains the feet of him that bringeth good tidings, that publisheth peace."
Nah. 1:15
Cf. Isa. 52:7

It is not pedicure that makes feet beautiful, not

the attentions of the chiropodist, but the errand
on which they are bent.

Here is a lovely picture of the fect of the evangelist, in which we have brought before us:

1. A gospel that is going somewhere.
    "Behold . . . the feet"—not the tongue,
    or the face, or the hands, but the feet.
2. A gospel from above.
    "Upon the mountains."
3. A gospel with the precise message which the
   world needs today.
    "That publisheth peace."

HABAKKUK

530. THE SLOGAN OF PROTESTANTISM

"The just shall live by his faith." HAB. 2:4

There are four emphases which may warrantably
be laid on this text, four of its words each of
which may be accented.

1. The just shall live by *faith.*
    That is the emphasis of Rom. 1:17.
2. The *just* shall live by faith.
    That is the emphasis of Gal. 3:11.
3. The just shall *live* by faith.
    That is the emphasis of Heb. 10:38.
4. The just *shall* live by faith.
    That is the emphasis of Hab. 2:4.

531. WAITING FOR THE VISION

*"For the vision is yet for an appointed time, but
at the end it shall speak, and not lie: though it
tarry, wait for it; because it will surely come, it
will not tarry."* HAB. 2:3

Why wait for the vision?

1. Because you cannot see where to go without it.
2. Because you cannot compel its coming, but must abide its leisure.
3. Because, if you do wait for it, it is certain to arrive at last.

532. THE PERILS OF THE MIDDLE PASSAGE

"O Lord, revive thy work in the midst of the years, in the midst of the years make known."

HAB. 3:2

The Northwest Passage is, as you know, the passage from the Atlantic to the Pacific, through the Arctic Ocean, across the north of North America. It was first made in 1850; but before the discoverer of 1850 pushed his way through, many had tried and failed. The Northwest Passage is a dangerous passage. Many a ship has been crushed and broken by the ice and many a sailor has been lost in the attempt to negotiate it.

It reminds me of the middle passage of life, a tract of experience fraught with special perils. What are they?

1. Loss of idealism
2. Loss of faith
3. Loss of the eternal

—J. D. Jones, *The Gospel of the Sovereignty*

533. THE HIDING OF HIS POWER

"There was the hiding of his power."

HAB. 3:4

It is not the habit of men to hide their power. Where they possess it, they display it. Not so God. Note:

1. He hides his power in nature.
   a) The force of gravitation
   b) Electricity
   c) Life itself
2. He hid his power in Christ.

"Is not this the carpenter?" No, the Creator!
3. He hides his power in the Church.
4. He hides his power in the heart.

ZEPHANIAH

534. THE LOVING SILENCES OF GOD
"He will be silent in his love." ZEPH. 3:17
R.S.V. Margin

Consider:
1. God's loving silence in respect of confessed and forsaken sin.
2. God's loving silence in regard to undeserved suffering.
3. God's loving silence in response to improper prayer.

HAGGAI

535. WHEN THINGS WORK OUT IN UNEXPECTED WAYS
"Ye looked for much, and, lo, it came to little." HAG. 1:9

These words describe the plight of those who, feverishly pursuing their own purposes, had neglected their religious obligations.

But the words have a wider reference. They portray an experience familiar to us all. We look for much, and, lo, there is but little.

1. Take it of the pleasures of sin.

217

2. Take it of our strongest and most strenuous endeavors.
3. It may also be true of our haunting fears.
   In such circumstances what are we to do?
   a) Face the situation as it is.
   b) Put right, so far as we can, any wrong that may account for it.
   c) Commit the matter to the Lord in prayer.
   d) Learn that only the spiritual truly satisfies.

536. A MAN OF THE RIGHT STAMP

"In that day . . . will [I] make thee as a signet."
HAG. 2:23

Some men are just rubber stamps—dittoes of others. Not so Zerubbabel. God planned to make him a man of mark, a personality creating an original and distinct impression.

What sort of person is that?

1. A man possessing authority.
   A signet suggests that.
2. A man easily identifiable.
   A signet intimates that.
3. A man begetting in others a sense of security.
   A signet implies that.

ZECHARIAH

537. PRIESTLY PREPARATION

"Now Joshua was clothed with filthy garments, and stood before the angel. And he answered and spake unto those that stood before him, saying, Take away the filthy garments from him. And unto him he said, Behold, I have caused thine iniquity to pass from thee, and I will clothe thee with change of raiment. And I said, Let them set

a *fair mitre upon his head. So they set a fair mitre upon his head."* ZECH. 3:3-5

Note three stages in the preparing of the high priest:

1. Cleansed
2. Clothed
3. Crowned

538. LEVELING THE MOUNTAIN

"Who art thou, O great mountain? before Zerubbabel thou shalt become a plain." ZECH. 4:7

How can we level the mountain? Here are a few ways:

1. The way of prayer
2. The way of taking someone into your confidence
3. The way of recalling past deliverances
   —W. J. Rowlands, *The Suburban Christ*

539. GOD BEGINNING SMALL

"Who hath despised the day of small things?"
ZECH. 4:10

"It is God's way," someone has said, "to begin small." You see that in nature. He does not start with the oak; he starts with the acorn. He does not start with the eagle; he starts with the egg. He does not start with the man; he starts with the baby. He begins small.

1. This was God's way at Bethlehem.
2. This was God's way at Pentecost.
3. This was God's way of building the Bible.
4. This is God's way of winning the world.
   "Modest beginnings are very good presages," says Matthew Henry.

540. THE NEW HUMANITY

ZECH. 8:5.

1. The new humanity is marked by youthfulness.

"Boys and girls"

2. The new humanity is characterized by enjoyment.
    "Playing"
3. The new humanity is on the move.
    "In the streets"
4. The new humanity is numerous.
    "Full"

—B. D. Johns

541. THE PIERCED HANDS

"And one shall say unto him, What are these wounds in thine hands? Then he shall answer, Those with which I was wounded in the house of my friends." Zech. 13:6

Those hands are:

1. Fountains of grace.
2. Titles of glory.
3. Seals of his power to save.

—W. Robertson Nicoll

542. THE TWILIGHT AND THE TRUE LIGHT

"And it shall come to pass in that day, that the light shall not be clear, nor dark: But it shall be one day which shall be known to the Lord, not day, nor night: but it shall come to pass that at evening time it shall be light." Zech. 14:6-7

1. Man's half-light.
    "Not clear, nor dark."
2. God's full light.
    "One day known to the Lord."
3. The light God gives to man.
    "At evening time it shall be light."

543. THE ONE LORD

"And the Lord shall be king over all the earth: in that day shall there be one Lord, and his name one." Zech. 14:9

1. The universality of the King's dominion.
    "Over all the earth."

2. The uniqueness of the King's supremacy
   "In that day there shall be one Lord."
3. The unity of the King's character
   "His name [that is, his character] one."
   —Daniel Hughes, *The Making of Man*

MALACHI

544. A BLESSED BURDEN

"*The burden of the word of the Lord.*"

MAL. 1:1

This is:

1. A burden of divine revelation.
2. A burden borne by the holiest of men.
3. A burden borne for the world.

—W. Osborne Lilley

545. WHOM TO PLEASE

"*Will he be pleased with thee?*" MAL. 1:8

1. Some please themselves.
2. Some seek to please others.
3. Some, eminently wise, strive to please God.

546. A STARTLING QUESTION

"*Where is the God of judgment?*"

MAL. 2:17

1. The question may be asked by the Christian in moments of distress.
2. The question may be asked by the wicked in their fancied security.
3. The question may be asked by the sceptic in his reluctant doubting.
4. The question will be answered by God:
   a) To the joy of the Christian.

b) To the confusion of the wicked.

c) To the satisfaction of the honest doubter.

d) To the full vindication of divine justice.

—W. Osborne Lilley

547. IN GOD'S REFINERY

"He shall sit as a refiner and purifier of silver."

MAL. 3:3

There is a saying attributed to Christ by Clement of Alexandria, not recorded in the four Gospels. "He that is near me is near the fire." Whether or not Jesus actually said that must be left an open question, but the sentence certainly does express one aspect of the truth concerning his impact on the souls of men. "He that is near me is near the fire." Is that so? "Yes," replies the prophet, "for he is like a refiner's fire . . . And he shall sit as a refiner and purifier of silver."

Let us go into God's refinery and see what we can discover there. What do you find?

1. You find the ore—great craggy lumps of raw human nature.

2. You find the crucible—the testing melting pot of circumstance.

3. You find the fire—the fierce flame of moral discipline.

4. You find the bellows—the rhythmic breathing of life.

5. You find the pure, gleaming metal—a stream of glowing beauty from which all dross has been purged away. To drop the figure, character fit for everlasting fellowship with a holy God.

548. CROWN JEWELS

"They shall be mine, saith the Lord of hosts, in that day when I make up my jewels."

MAL. 3:17

Consider:
1. The jewel finding.
2. The jewel grinding.
3. The jewel setting.

—T. De Witt Talmage

549. JEWELS OF GOD

"They shall be mine, saith the Lord of hosts, in that day when I make up my jewels."

MAL. 3:17

Note that jewels are:
1. Treasured.
2. Preserved and guarded.
3. Used on great occasions.
4. Sometimes counterfeited.

—Unknown

550. THE SOLAR CHRIST

"But unto you that fear my name shall the Sun of righteousness arise with healing in his wings."

MAL. 4:2

Consider that Christ is the Sun of righteousness:
1. In his uniqueness.
2. In his centralness.
3. In his brightness.
4. In his fulness.
5. In his everlastingness.

INDEX OF SCRIPTURE

(References are to Outline Numbers.)

INDEX OF AUTHORS
AND SUBJECTS

(References are to Outline Numbers.)

237

ACKNOWLEDGMENTS

The author expresses appreciation to the following publishers for permission to outline sermons from their publications:

Carey Kingsgate Press for W. G. Branch's "The Land of Big Things" from *In the Days of Thy Youth.*

James Clarke & Co. Ltd. for G. T. Bellhouse's "When God Becomes Real" from *Our Sufficient Beauty*; H. L. Simpson's "The Conquest of the Cup" from *Communion Addresses*; and J. Wither's "Eternity in the Heart," "The Orthopaedic Gospel," "The Whispering Chambers of the Imagination," "Jonah's Fare" from *Speak for Yourself.*

T. & T. Clark for H. R. Mackintosh's "The Burden-bearing Lord," "An Ideal Friendship," and "Preoccupied" from his *Sermons*; James S. Stewart's "God's Glory in the Morning," from *The Strong Name*, and "Why Be a Christian?" from *The Gates of New Life*. For the following from *Expository Times*: Tom Dick's "The Prodigal Parent"; Lynn Harold Hough's "The Drawings of the Divine"; G. Johnstone Jeffrey's "Meddling with God"; J. Ithel Jones's "The Darkness of Doubt"; Stuart McWilliam's "Silence and a Voice"; James Munn's "God's Bounty for Another Year"; R. Leonard Small's "Our Attitude to Tragedy."

The Committee on Publications of the Church of Scotland for D. M. Baillie's "God Carrying His People" and "What to Boast About" from *Out of Nazareth.*

Wm. B. Eerdmans Publishing Co. for Stephen Olford's "At the Crossroads" from *Christianity and You* and G. B. Duncan's "The Walled Garden" from *Wanting the Impossible.*

239

The Epworth Press for G. T. Bellhouse's "The Secret of Happiness" from *The Hand of Glory* and "Blessed Advice" from *Immortal Longing*; Wilfred Shepherd's "The Ministry of Protection" from *Noughts and Crosses*; W. E. Sangster's "Counsel in a Crisis" from *The Craft of Sermon Construction*, "Holy—but Stained" from *Westminster Sermons*, Vol. I, and "The Ministry of Protection" from *The Craft of the Sermon*.

Harper & Brothers for G. H. Morrison's "The Ministry of Interruption," "The Outlook of the Optimist," "The Bow in the Cloud," "The Choked Wells," "The Ladder of Prayer" from *The Incomparable Christ*; R. W. Sockman's "In and Out" and "The Arm of the Lord" from *The Unemployed Carpenter*.

Hodder & Stoughton Ltd. for James Denney's "The Great Charter" from *The Way Everlasting*; J. D. Jones's "On the Slope," "The Divided Heart," "The Sovereignty of God," "The Zeal of the Lord," "The Perils of the Middle Passage" from *The Gospel of the Sovereignty*; J. H. Jowett's "Ascending the Hill of the Lord"; M. E. Macdonald's "The Meaning of the Sacrament" from *The Vitality of Faith*; G. H. Morrison's "The Bow in the Cloud," "The Choked Wells," "The Ladder of Prayer," "The Ministry of Interruption," "The Outlook of the Optimist" from *The Incomparable Christ*.

Kregel Publications, Grand Rapids 6, Michigan, for F. E. Marsh's "The Atmosphere," "The Wind," "The Dove," "God as Fire" from *Emblems of the Holy Spirit*.

James Nisbet and Company, Limited for H. H. Farmer's "Vows" from *The Healing Cross*.

Pickering & Inglis Ltd. for H. Y. Pickering's "Reasons for Returning" and James Smith's "David's Offering," "The Chosen Tree," "The Cheapest Market" from *Handfuls on Purpose*.

Charles Scribner's Sons for H. H. Farmer's "Vows" from *The Healing Cross*.

The Sunday School Board of the Southern Baptist Convention for W. W. Week's "The Coming of the Dreamer," "Compromises," "Hedged," "Harmonies," and "Overdone and Underdone" from *The Face of Christ*.